1975

LIVING IN THE SEVENTIES

2SM 2SM
EYEWITNESS NEWS
EYEWITNESS NEWS

FOREWORD

I turned 12 and started high school in Canberra in 1975, so it is a year of many formative memories for me. For those who were 'living in the seventies', our stories might reference Ford Cortinas, Skyhooks songs, the North Melbourne Kangaroos taking home the VFL premiership, *Number 96* (no, I wasn't allowed to watch it!) and, of course, the Dismissal of Prime Minister Gough Whitlam on 11 November.

These memories and more are all captured within the National Library of Australia's collection—the largest in the world focusing on Australia and its people. By holding these stories—in manuscripts, books, magazines, ephemera, pictures, posters, music and art—we help Australians understand and remember our past, make sense of our present day and imagine our future. For those of us 'here' in 1975, the stories will chime with our own memories. For the many Australians born or arriving in Australia in the last 50 years—and there are twice as many Australians in 2025 as in 1975—I hope the stories in the Library's collection will solve some puzzles, provide new insights and elicit many an 'aha' moment.

The seventies are often characterised as a decade of expansion and transformation. There was the advancement of technology, changing social movements and expectations, political disruption and change, and the arrival of cult icons that remain in the Australian collective memory 50 years on.

In 1975 colour had arrived in the form of new television sets, tight satin shirts and flared jeans were fashion favourites, and Daryl Braithwaite was the King of Pop. A new wave of Australian cinema saw an adaption of *Picnic at Hanging Rock* grace the screen, a film that 50 years on is still influential for contemporary cinephiles. In sport, Evonne Goolagong, a Wiradjuri woman, and John Newcombe both won the 1975 Australian Open, the last time that two Australians have done so simultaneously.

In the political sphere, major migration to Australia shifted from Europe to Asia, in part due to the endorsement of a multicultural Australia by the Whitlam government, as well as the end of the Vietnam War. Activists from the women's liberation movement were drawing attention to gender inequality and campaigning for reproductive autonomy. On March 8 more than 5,000 people marched for International Women's Day. The campaign by the Gurindji people for the return of their homelands came to fruition, after an official strike that had started in 1966. This led to the development of land rights legislation for Aboriginal and Torres Strait Islander peoples by the federal government.

This book is a companion to our exhibition *1975: Living in the Seventies*, which features more than 200 items that honour pop icons, bonzer fashion, political movers and shakers, and protest movements, both pro-equality and anti-war, along with everyday slices of 1970s life. The exhibition offers a nostalgic trip back to a seminal decade in Australian social and political history, both for those who experienced it and those who want to learn about it.

The people, places and events captured in the collection are all part of our national story. I invite you to explore the Library's chronicle of Australian life in the seventies and reflect on how our world has changed in the 50 years since.

Dr Marie-Louise Ayres FAHA
Director-General,
National Library of Australia

UNKNOWN PHOTOGRAPHER, *Gough Whitlam speaking on the steps of Parliament House*, 1975

EGO IS NOT A DIRTY WORD

Words and Music by
GREG MACAINSH

Recorded by
Skyhooks
on Mushroom Records

GREG

1975: LIVING IN THE SEVENTIES

In the classic Australian hit song from the seventies, *Horror Movie*, singer 'Shirley' Strachan describes the experience of watching a horror movie on television only to discover he is really watching 'the six-thirty news'. Strachan delivered the twist at the end of the song by suggesting, in his characteristic working-class drawl, that all was not right in the world. The song was released by Australia's favourite glam rock band, Skyhooks, in December 1974. It went to the top of the charts in early 1975. The album on which it featured, *Living in the 70's*, became the highest-selling Australian record of that time, with sales of more than 250,000 copies. *Horror Movie*'s iconic status was confirmed when it was selected to be the opening song for the first colour episode (screened on 1 March 1975) of *Countdown*, which was then one of Australia's most popular television shows.

What was it that made Strachan liken the seventies to the experience of watching a horror movie? Mid-decade news broadcasts were filled with stories of disasters and political crises. On Christmas Day 1974 Darwin was hit by Cyclone Tracy. Wind gusts of more than 200 kilometres per hour destroyed over 80 per cent of Darwin and killed 66 people. The new year saw the grim task of evacuation and recovery begin. The news did not improve when, on 5 January 1975, the bulk carrier SS *Lake Illawarra* collided with the Tasman Bridge in Hobart, collapsing its central span. Five cars plummeted into the Derwent River below and the *Lake Illawarra* sank within minutes of the accident. Twelve people died in the catastrophic collision.

GREG MACAINSH (b. 1950), *Ego Is Not a Dirty Word*, 1975

Hobart was split in two, with residents of the eastern shore of the Derwent isolated from the main part of the city, as the long process of rebuilding the bridge got under way. The bridge would not reopen until October 1977.

International news was also filled with history-making stories. In 1974 the world watched as the Watergate scandal unfolded in the United States, culminating in the resignation of the embattled President Richard Nixon. Governments around the world grappled with 'stagflation' (simultaneous stagnant economic growth and high inflation) and an energy crisis, as the price of oil rapidly rose. In the early months of 1975 the news also focused on the recent offensive by the North Vietnamese in the Vietnam War. Australian combat cameraman Neil Davis was there to document the moment when a Soviet-made T-54 tank smashed through the gates of the Presidential Palace in Saigon on 30 April 1975, signalling the capitulation of the South Vietnamese Government. Revolutions and conflicts erupted around the globe as the long tail of colonisation in Africa and Asia continued to unfold. When the 'Carnation Revolution' in Portugal toppled the Estado Novo regime and installed a new government in 1974, the country's colonies, including Mozambique and Angola, became independent. As the Portuguese withdrew from East Timor, the East Timorese people briefly experienced independence, only to have the Indonesian army invade and annex the territory in December 1975. East Timor would not fully regain independence until May 2002, when it became the Democratic Republic of Timor-Leste.

Australian politics was also riven with drama in 1974 and 1975. The Whitlam government narrowly survived a double dissolution election on 18 May 1974. This set the scene for a historic joint sitting of parliament in August 1974, which passed key legislation, including the creation of two Senate seats each for the Australian Capital Territory and the Northern Territory, and the establishment of Medibank, a public health insurance scheme for all Australians. Reforms continued in February 1975 with the introduction of a new Australian honours system, replacing the imperial system.

STEWART MCCRAE (1919–2008), *'Can't you think of something except "It's sink or swim"?'*, 1970s

In June 1975 parliament passed the *Racial Discrimination Act*, outlawing discrimination on the basis of race, and the *Family Law Act*, which created the Family Court of Australia and provided for no-fault divorce. The government also passed the *Great Barrier Reef Marine Park Act 1975*, which provided for the protection of the Great Barrier Reef.

The Whitlam government was also responding to the demands of the women's liberation movement. The strength and vibrancy of the movement in Australia was seen on International Women's Day on 8 March 1975, when more than 5,000 people marched from the Domain to Sydney Town Hall. Activists were calling for better access to contraception, sex education and abortion rights and campaigning against discrimination in the workplace. They also wanted to draw attention to the endemic problems of sexual and domestic violence. A key leader in the movement was Dr Anne Summers, the author of *Damned Whores and God's Police*, the classic feminist history of how women's roles in society had been stereotyped. In 1974 Summers and other activists occupied two vacant houses in Sydney and established the Elsie Women's Refuge Night Shelter. In January 1975 the Whitlam government provided one-off funding for the shelter, and by the end of the year more shelters had been set up in cities around Australia. The Whitlam government also appointed Elizabeth Reid as Women's Advisor to the Prime Minister, the first such position in the world. Reid helped push for equal pay for women, paid maternity leave in the public service, benefits for single mothers and the funding of community childcare centres. She also led the Australian delegation to the United Nation's World Conference of the International Women's Year, held in Mexico in June–July 1975.

The 1970s was also a decade of rapid change in Australia's attitude to migration. The Whitlam government articulated a new vision for a multicultural Australia in which migrants from diverse cultural backgrounds were celebrated for their contribution to Australian society. The migrant intake began to become more diverse, particularly with the influx of refugees from Vietnam, Laos and Cambodia after the end of the Vietnam War. Political unrest and conflict in East Timor, South America and the Middle East also prompted many to seek protection in Australia.

1975 saw the culmination of the campaign for land rights for the Gurindji people at Daguragu (Wattie Creek) in the Northern Territory. What became known as the 'Wave Hill Walk-Off' began as a strike by Indigenous pastoral workers on Wave Hill cattle station for better pay and conditions in 1966 and evolved into a struggle for land rights that would dominate Australian politics for years to come. In 1967 Gurindji Elder Vincent Lingiari petitioned Governor-General Lord Casey for land to be returned to Indigenous ownership. The campaign gathered strength, with support from activists including the writer Frank Hardy, who helped organise protests in Melbourne and Sydney. In 1971 Lingiari, Galarrwuy Yunupingu and Ted Egan released the single *The Gurindji Blues*, which sold 20,000 copies. The strike continued until 1975, when the Whitlam government negotiated an agreement with the owner of Wave Hill Station, Lord Vestey, to lease 3,236 square kilometres to the Gurindji people. On 16 August 1975 Indigenous photographer Mervyn Bishop captured the moment when Prime Minister Gough Whitlam poured a handful of red dirt into Vincent Lingiari's hands at a ceremony at Daguragu, symbolising the return of the land to Gurindji ownership. This successful campaign would be the first step towards the development by the federal government of land rights legislation for Indigenous Australians.

Further north, self-determination was also being returned to the first nations people of Papua New Guinea. The Australian Government had administered the former British territories of Papua from 1906 and of New Guinea from 1945. On 9 September 1975 the *Papua New Guinea Independence Act* received Royal Assent and, a week later, in a ceremony attended by HRH Prince Charles, Michael Somare was sworn in as Papua New Guinea's first prime minister.

While the Whitlam government was implementing its program of reforms, it also found itself mired in a rolling series of political controversies. One story that dominated the media for much of 1975 was the so-called 'loans affair', in which the Minister for Minerals and Energy 'Rex' Connor engaged a mysterious London-based Pakastani commodities dealer, Tirath Khemlani, to negotiate a massive loan to invest in developing Australian mineral and energy resources. When Khemlani failed to provide any evidence of progress in sourcing the money, the government withdrew Connor's permission to seek the loan. However, after news leaked out that Connor had continued to liaise with Khemlani, Whitlam dismissed him from the Cabinet for misleading parliament. The opposition, led by Malcolm Fraser, used the loans affair to argue that the government had acted improperly. This controversy, combined with rising inflation, unemployment and economic stagnation, provided the pretext for the opposition to block the government's budget in the Senate. The deadlock in the Senate was dramatically broken on 11 November when Governor-General Sir John Kerr controversially sacked Whitlam's government and commissioned Liberal leader Malcolm Fraser as caretaker prime minister. A federal election held shortly afterwards, on 13 December, confirmed the Fraser government in office. While political power was transferred peacefully at the election, Kerr's dismissal of Whitlam was seen by many as a serious break of constitutional convention that had seriously damaged Australian democracy. On the day of his dismissal Whitlam denounced Kerr's actions in one of the most famous speeches in Australian political history, made on the steps of the parliament: 'Well may we say "God save the Queen" because nothing will save the Governor-General'.

While 1975 is often remembered for the political disruption of 'the Dismissal', it was also an incredibly vibrant time for music, film, television and sport. In addition to Skyhooks' dominance of the charts, many other Australian artists were finding success. Bands Sherbet and Hush, and singers John Paul Young, Daryl Braithwaite,

UNKNOWN PHOTOGRAPHER, *Malcolm Fraser at Parliament House, Canberra, 1975*

Olivia Newton-John and Marcia Hines, were all on the way to becoming household names. An appearance on *Countdown*, with an endorsement from the program's host Ian 'Molly' Meldrum, ensured a hit would follow. Live appearances—often lip-synced—or music videos were the show's staple. Families across Australia gathered in their loungerooms every Sunday night at 6pm to watch appearances by international artists such as Rod Stewart, Status Quo, Queen and ABBA. This helped create a soundtrack for a generation, which can still be heard today on the radio.

1975 was also a great time for blockbuster movies. New releases were major cultural events that reached mass audiences in a way that is hard to imagine today. Steven Spielberg's *Jaws* left an indelible mark on popular culture. The story of a great white shark preying on holiday-makers at Martha's Vineyard in Massachusetts struck a chord with beach-loving Australians. While most of the movie was shot on location, underwater footage of live sharks was filmed at Dangerous Reef in South Australia. For a generation of adolescent Australians, watching *Jaws* meant that they would carry a fear of being eaten alive in the surf for the rest of their lives. It would become the highest-grossing movie of all time—until surpassed by a new blockbuster, *Star Wars*, in 1977. Another film that had a major impact on young Australians was *The Rocky Horror Picture Show*, an adaptation of the original 1973 musical of the same name. Combining both horror and science fiction genres, it was a tale of a young married couple whose car broke down on a stormy night, forcing them to take refuge in a gothic mansion. Pandemonium ensued. Punctuated with catchy songs and amazing dance routines, this modern take on Mary Shelley's *Frankenstein* would go on to become a cult classic shown at late-night sessions in cinemas. *Monty Python and the Holy Grail* was another movie that became part of the zeitgeist with its surreal send-up of an Arthurian quest. For decades after the film's release, teenagers in anglophone countries around the world would compete to recite scenes from the movie verbatim, while family members rolled their eyes.

The early seventies also saw a 'new wave' of Australian cinema achieve critical acclaim and popular success. *Picnic at Hanging Rock*, a mysterious costume drama set in 1900 in which a group of schoolgirls disappear on a bush walk, helped establish Peter Weir's reputation as one of Australia's most successful film directors. The film's haunting soundtrack and ambiguous ending provided an ideal conversation starter for 1970s dinner parties. Guests could endlessly debate what happened to the girls and what it meant. The mid-seventies was also a time when it was fashionable to celebrate Australian working-class culture. Jack Thompson's portrayal of Foley, the hard-drinking 'gun' shearer, in *Sunday Too Far Away*, provided the classic depiction of a good bloke trying to make his way in the world. With its affectionate depiction of male mateship, binge drinking and brawling, *Sunday Too Far Away* reminds us of how much Australia has changed in the last 50 years.

While Jack Thompson was the personification of the Australian working-class male on the big screen, Paul Hogan became the representation of the everyman on the small screen. Starting in 1973, *The Paul Hogan Show* provided a weekly dose of sketch comedy featuring Hogan and his sidekick 'Strop' (played by Hogan's manager, John Cornell). A mixture of slapstick, sexism and larrikinism, *The Paul Hogan Show* was originally broadcast on Channel 7 and then Channel 9, running until 1984. Hogan was also the celebrity brand behind the ubiquitous cigarette advertising campaign 'Anyhow, have a Winfield'. His smiling face, along with a requisite pack of Winfield Reds, could be seen everywhere in print, television and billboards. Hogan's personification of all things Australian would continue into the 1980s, when he became the face of the successful Australian Tourism Commission campaign 'Throw another shrimp on the barbie', and as the fictional character Mick Dundee in the 1986 hit movie *Crocodile Dundee*.

In contrast to Hogan's populist entertainment, the Australian Broadcasting Commission (later Corporation) was a haven for more experimental comedy, producing programs such as *The Aunty Jack Show* and *The Norman Gunston Show*. *Aunty Jack* was set in the industrial city of Wollongong and featured a violent cross-dressing 'aunty' (played by Grahame Bond), who wore a boxing glove and football boots, and regularly threatened to 'rip yer bloody arms off'. It was unlike any other show on Australian television. *The Norman Gunston Show* featured a fictional talk show host played by Garry McDonald, who confused international celebrities with his extravagant Brylcreemed comb-over, shaving cuts and ill-fitting suits. Gunston's seemingly naive, yet pointed, questions neatly skewered his interviewees, leaving them agog or in fits of laughter. Both programs reflected an affectionate, but also sardonic, take on Australian culture, while providing a surreal commentary on the mainstays of commercial television, including soap operas such as *Number 96* and *The Sullivans*, and late-night shows such as *The Graham Kennedy Show* and *The Ernie Sigley Show*.

While Australians loved television, they also loved their sport, and 1975 was a great year for sport. It had not yet become the entertainment business that would emerge in the 1980s, but the early signs were there. In winter, Australians were still very much obsessed with Australian Rules football and rugby league. Soccer had strong support among migrant communities and was just beginning to cross over into the mainstream, thanks mainly to the Socceroos having qualified for the 1974 FIFA World Cup. For Australian Rules fans, it was the Victorian Football League (VFL) that dominated. North Melbourne finally broke its jinx by winning the grand final in 1975 against Hawthorn, making it the last of the league's 12 teams to win a VFL premiership.

In rugby league, it was the New South Wales Rugby League that attracted the biggest stars with its traditional 12-team Sydney-based competition. The 1975 grand final saw a clash between rivals St George and Eastern Suburbs. In a sign of the creeping commercialism entering the game, St George fullback Graeme Langlands sparked a controversy when he wore white boots—as opposed to the traditional black—as part of a sponsorship deal he had with Adidas. Such attention-seeking behaviour was unheard of in rugby league and, in a measure of karmic justice, St George was thrashed by Eastern Suburbs 30–0.

On the tennis court, Australians were dominating international competitions. Evonne Goolagong (Cawley), a Wiradjuri woman, won the 1975 Australian Open by defeating Martina Navratilova 6–3, 6–2 in the final. John Newcombe became the men's champion in the same tournament when he overcame American champion Jimmy Connors 7–5, 3–6, 6–4, 7–6.

UNKNOWN PHOTOGRAPHER, *World champion Heather McKay playing a forehand drive during a squash match in Canberra*, 1972

Australia hosted the charismatic West Indies cricket team for the summer. The series was notable for the destruction wrought by Australian fast bowlers Dennis Lillee and Jeff Thomson, both of whom could bowl at over 150 kilometres per hour. Australia won the series 5–1, but 'the Windies', as they were universally known, had learned the lesson of the power of fast bowling and would return in future series with their own blistering bowling attack.

The success of the Windies' tour attracted the attention of media magnate Kerry Packer. When the Australian Cricket Board rejected his 1976 bid for the broadcast rights, Packer responded by establishing the World Series Cricket competition a year later. After two seasons of parallel international competitions, a compromise was negotiated—and Packer achieved his goal of obtaining the broadcast rights for cricket. This was a major step towards the professionalisation and commercialisation of Australian sport. Competitions that had been parochial and suburban for decades began to be transformed into the major national sports businesses that we know today.

When we look back to 1975, it is tempting to view Australia through a haze of nostalgia. You can still hear classic 'hits of the seventies' on the radio, watch the iconic TV shows on *YouTube* and laugh at pictures of outrageous moustaches, white silk shirts and flared jeans. But is there more to this year than a dose of boomer nostalgia? Looking at the collections held by the National Library of Australia reveals a much more complex story.

1975 was a year when Australia was in transition. Its economy was undergoing fundamental change, with increasing reliance on the mining sector. The flow of migrants coming to Australia had begun to shift from Europe to Asia. The White Australia policy, which had been slowly dismantled over the previous decade, was finally gone, replaced with a commitment to multiculturalism by both the Whitlam and Fraser governments. The women's liberation movement had challenged many long-held assumptions about the roles of women in Australian society. The establishment of women's refuges and no-fault divorce were important first steps in addressing deep injustices in Australian society. Our colonial legacy, and particularly the dispossession of Indigenous Australians, was now firmly on the political agenda. While the year ended with the dismissal of the Whitlam government, reforms would continue through the late 1970s and into the 1980s.

Change was not limited to politics and economics. Australian popular culture was also reinventing itself. By the mid-1970s there was an increasingly confident cohort of performers, writers, filmmakers, television producers and artists producing a distinctly Australian take on the world. The nation had begun to tell its own stories. The cultural cringe that had defined our attitude to the world in the 1950s and 1960s was beginning to fade. Australia was now a much prouder and more assertive nation. Skyhooks captured this new cultural confidence with their second hit album for 1975: *Ego Is Not a Dirty Word*. Like the band, Australia had begun to embrace its own distinct style and celebrate its place in the sun.

Dr Guy Hansen
Director, Exhibitions
National Library of Australia

GOOD VIBES

Our collective memory of 1975 is populated with celebrities, songs, television shows, cooking fads and fashion trends. Television, which had just started transmitting in colour in Australia, saturated popular culture. Talk shows, serials, music shows, comedies and advertisements were watched by nearly everyone, providing a shared set of cultural touchstones.

On the radio, Australia's favourite glam rock band, Skyhooks, dominated with two hit albums, while Swedish pop group ABBA topped the charts. Flared jeans, platform shoes and bright colours ruled fashion tastes.

1970 1971 1972 1973 1974 1975 1976 1977 1978 1979

'Be in it today, live more of your life'

The Victorian Government began the health promotion and advertising campaign 'Life. Be in it.' in 1975. Television cartoons featured people doing a range of activities. The main character was Norm, a middle-aged man with a prominent beer belly. The campaign went national in 1978.

ALEX STITT (1937–2016), *Life. Be in it.*, 1977

Sheet music

In the 1970s the popular music charts were based on the sale of vinyl singles, which featured an A and a B side. There were also charts for the sale of albums, or LPs (long-play records) as they were known. Sales were driven by how often records were played on AM radio stations. Popular songs were often published as sheet music, usually available in the same stores that sold the record.

AC/DC

One of the most influential Australian bands to emerge in 1975 was AC/DC. Founded by brothers Angus and Malcolm Young, the band released its debut album, *High Voltage*, in February 1975, followed by *T.N.T.* in December.

BON SCOTT (1946–1980); MALCOLM YOUNG (1953–2017); ANGUS YOUNG (b. 1955), *High Voltage*, 1975

Olivia Newton-John

In the mid-seventies Olivia Newton-John had a string of country and pop hits in Australia, England and the United States. In 1978 she co-starred with John Travolta in the musical *Grease*. She is one of the bestselling female Australian artists of all time.

JOHN ROSTILL (1942–1973), *If You Love Me (Let Me Know), performed by Olivia Newton-John*, 1974

Mock opera

British rock group Queen topped the Australian charts in 1975 with their six-minute rock epic *Bohemian Rhapsody*. Part of the song's success was due to its video clip, which captured the charisma of lead singer Freddie Mercury and was perfect for use on music shows such as *Countdown*.

FREDDIE MERCURY (1946–1991), *Bohemian Rhapsody*, c. 1975

Scandi pop

ABBA's single *Mamma Mia* spent 10 weeks at number one in the Australian popular music charts in 1975. It was one of several Australian hits for the Swedish pop group. Following their early success in Australia, ABBA went on to experience major international acclaim.

BENNY ANDERSSON (b. 1946); STIG ANDERSON (1931–1997); BJÖRN ULVAEUS (b. 1945), *Mamma Mia*, c. 1975

Sherbet

From 1972 to 1978 Sherbet was one of Australia's most successful bands. Its lead singer, Daryl Braithwaite, was voted King of Pop in 1975, 1976 and 1977. Braithwaite regularly co-hosted *Countdown* with Molly Meldrum. Sherbet's 1976 hit *Howzat* went to number one in Australia and New Zealand, as well as charting in the United Kingdom and South Africa.

UNKNOWN PHOTOGRAPHER, *Sherbet*, c. 1976

Marcia Hines

Marcia Hines came to Australia from the United States in 1970 to appear in Harry M. Miller's production of the US musical *Hair*. In 1973 she played the role of Mary Magdalene in *Jesus Christ Superstar*, confirming her place as a major new talent.

In 1975 Hines toured with the Daly-Wilson Big Band and had her first solo hit with a cover of James Taylor's *Fire and Rain*.

PETER KELLY (b. 1949), *Marcia Hines with Australia's Daly-Wilson Big Band on international tour, 1975*

'A voice to remember'

Singer-songwriter Kandiah Kamalesvaran, better known as Kamahl, toured Australia in 1975 after winning Australian Record of the Year for 1974. He also toured Europe and the United States. One of his 1975 releases, *The Elephant Song*, was a number one hit in the Netherlands and reached number three in Sweden.

CAMINI PTY LTD, *Kamahl: 1975 Australian Tour*, 1975

The Jays

Double Jay Rock, the first Australian Broadcasting Commission youth radio station, began broadcasting at 1540 kHz on AM radio in Sydney at 11 am on Sunday 19 January 1975. The first record to be played was Skyhooks' *You Just Like Me 'Cos I'm Good in Bed*, a song which had been banned from commercial networks owing to its overt sexual content. Double Jay would later evolve into the national FM youth network Triple J.

UNKNOWN ARTIST, *Double Jay Rock '1540'*, 1978

Courtesy the National Film and Sound Archive, Copyright Australian Broadcasting Corporation

DOUBLE JAY
ROCK
1540

AUSTRALIA

Molly

Ian 'Molly' Meldrum was the talent coordinator for *Countdown*, a weekly review of popular music featuring live performances and music videos. He had previously worked as a record producer and music journalist and, after joining *Countdown*, became one of the most influential voices in the Australian music industry. An endorsement from Meldrum, and an opportunity to perform on *Countdown*, could help guarantee success in the charts.

RENNIE ELLIS (1940–2003), *Ian 'Molly' Meldrum, Prahran*, 1978

Ego

After the chart-topping success of Skyhooks' debut album, *Living in the 70's*, they quickly released their second album *Ego Is Not a Dirty Word*. The album's two singles—the title track and *All My Friends Are Getting Married*—became classics of 70s Aussie rock.

GREG MACAINSH (composer, b. 1950); NEIL CURTIS (album art, 1950–2006), *Ego Is Not a Dirty Word*, 1975

farewell Aunty Jack
Words and music
by Grahame Bond
Recorded
by
Aunty Jack
and
Thin Arthur
on
Picture
Records
Pty
Limited.
60¢
PICTURE RECORD PUBLISHING.
18 Gladesville Road, Hunters Hill, N.S.W., Australia.

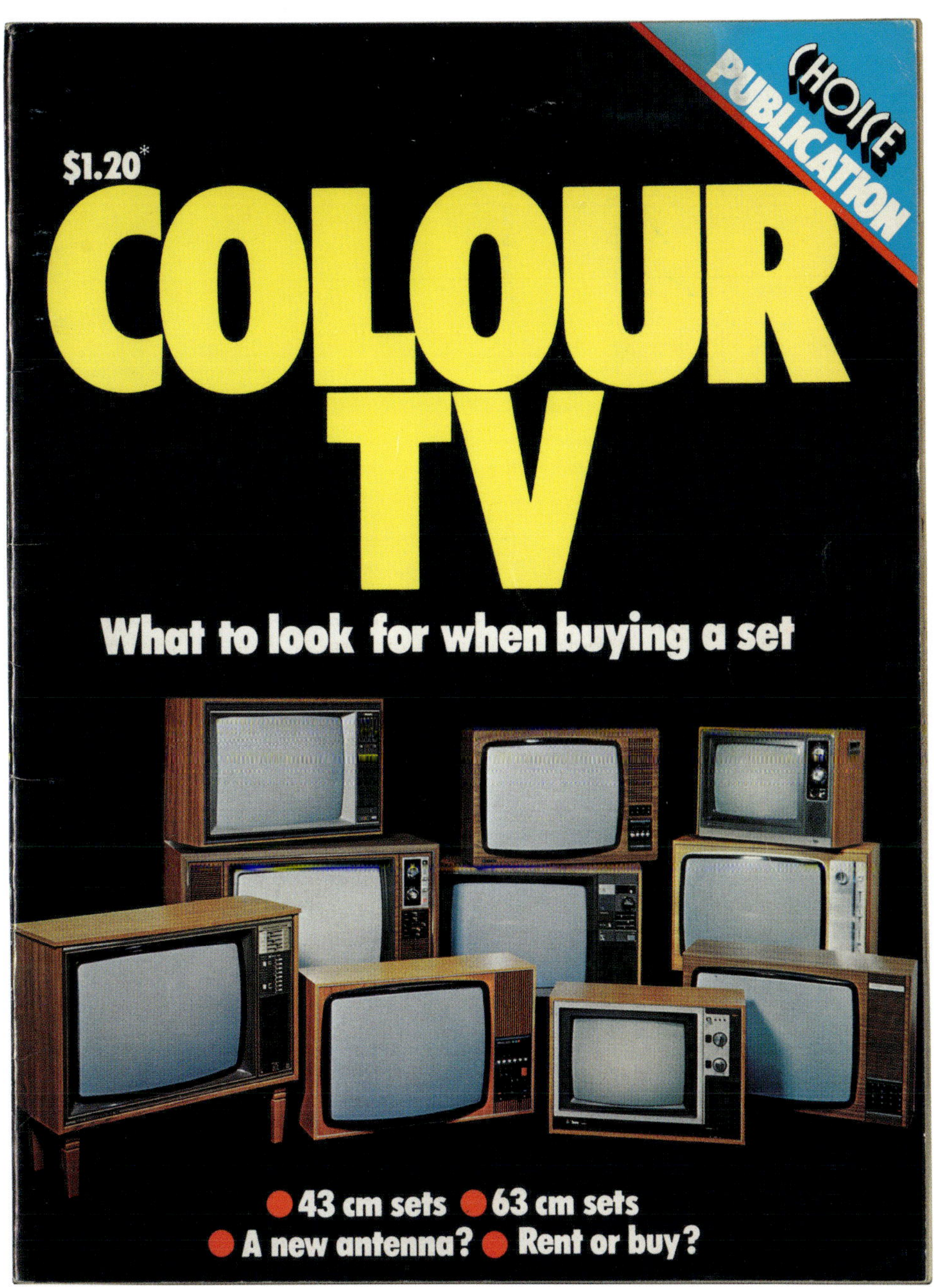

Aunty Jack

The Aunty Jack Show was set in the industrial city of Wollongong and starred Grahame Bond as a violent cross-dressing 'aunty', who wore a single boxing glove and football boots. It was unlike any other show on Australian television. The lilting song played at the end of each episode encouraged viewers to tune in again next week—or else Aunty Jack would 'rip yer bloody arms off'.

GRAHAME BOND (b. 1943), *Farewell Aunty Jack*, c. 1974

In glorious colour

Colour television was introduced to Australia on 1 March 1975. The new transmission format opened up a market for colour televisions. The sets cost more than $1,000, the equivalent of approximately $8,800 in today's money. The many who could not afford to upgrade their sets continued to watch in black and white.

AUSTRALIAN CONSUMERS ASSOCIATION, *Colour TV: What to Look for When Buying a Set*, 1977

TV Week

In 1971 *TV Week* had a national circulation of 400,000 readers. In addition to providing a weekly program schedule, the magazine also ran background features and photo shoots relating to popular television programs and personalities.

FRANK COOK (editor), *TV Week*, 1975

A yoga first

Long before Richard Simmons' fitness show, Jane Fonda's workout videos and today's online influencers, Swami Sarasvati presented a yoga instructional show on Australian morning television. Titled simply *Swami*, it ran from 1968 to 1978 and helped popularise yoga in Australia.

SWAMI SARASVATI (c. 1941–2023), *Enjoy Living through Yoga*, 1975

ENJOY LIVING
through
YOGA

The Time Lord

Tom Baker's first of seven seasons playing Doctor Who was broadcast in 1975. His eccentric interpretation of the character, who wore a ludicrously long scarf and liberally distributed jelly babies, proved an instant hit. Baker's first season featured all-time classic stories and villains such as the Daleks, the Cybermen and the Sontarans.

UNKNOWN PHOTOGRAPHER, *Tom Baker as Doctor Who*, c. 1974–81

The Gold Logie

The most prestigious award in Australian television in the 1970s was the Gold Logie, presented for Most Popular Personality. Denise Drysdale won the award for best female performer in 1975 and 1976. Garry McDonald also received the award as Norman Gunston in 1976, becoming the first fictional character to win a Gold Logie. The awards were voted on by viewers, who sent in coupons from *TV Week* magazine.

BRUCE POSTLE (b. 1940), *Norman Gunston and Denise Drysdale at the Logie Awards presentation night, each with their Gold Logie*, 1976

What's for dinner?

The seventies were a time of great experimentation and change. Metric units of measurement became standard in 1971. Chest freezers were popular as people tried to beat the price rises due to inflation. Tropical fruits were popular and who could forget all those jellied dishes?

'No watch, no worry cooking'

The Monier Crock-Pot was an electric slow-cooking pot for 'career girls and working wives' and Margaret Fulton's recipe book was supplied with each purchase: 'switch it on low, before leaving for work, then a perfect dinner awaits your homecoming'. While slow cookers had become popular from the 1940s, when many women began working outside the home, the Crock-Pot was a US brand first introduced to Australia in the early 1970s.

MARGARET FULTON (1924–2019), *The Margaret Fulton Crock-Pot Cookbook*, 1976

DIANA WYNNE (editor, 1934–2011), *When the Boss Comes to Dinner*, c. 1975

BABETTE HAYES (b. 1938), *Party Fare*, 1970

THE SOUTH AUSTRALIA COUNTRY WOMEN'S ASSOCIATION, *Calendar of Meat and Fish Recipes*, 1975

BERNARD KING (1934–2002), *Bernard King's Spring Cookbook*, 1977

Recipes 1975, 1975

The House of Tarvydas

Born in postwar Germany to Lithuanian parents, Ruth Tarvydas emigrated with her family to Western Australia in 1949. At age 19, she and her brother Harvey were responsible for introducing boutique culture to Perth, opening The House of Tarvydas on Hay Street. They soon launched the fashion label 'Ruta', which focused on exciting trends for the youth market. In the 1970s the boutique moved to larger premises, which included accessory stores, a cafe and enough space to hold fashion parades. Tarvydas later became the first Australian designer to export clothing overseas.

BRUCE HOWARD (b. 1936), *Ruth Tarvydas, Perth, Western Australia*, c. 1975

A flair for flares

With origins as durable and functional workwear, denim soon found its way into mainstream fashion and is regarded as a symbol of self-expression. In the 1970s jeans were high-waisted, blue or scrubbed, straight-legged or flared, and could be decorated with embroidery or trims—whatever the wearer desired.

STERLING CLOTHING PTY LTD, *'Colonials have a flair for the leggy look: easy living, long lasting jeans'*, c. 1970–75

BACK IN THE DAY

Looking back from the 21st century, 1975 can seem both familiar and different. In Australia, postwar migration and the baby boom had boosted the population towards 14 million. Most Australians lived in cities and relied on cars for transport. The majority of the population was of European descent, with large-scale migration from Asia and Africa only just beginning.

The mining boom, which had started in the 1960s, continued to gain momentum. Movies, radio, television, sport and live music provided much of the entertainment for this growing population. Computers and satellite technology were just beginning to be used in the workplace and at home, with the full impact of information technology still to come.

Sunday Too Far Away

One of actor Jack Thompson's first starring roles was his portrayal of gun shearer Foley in this searing depiction of 1950s itinerant shearers on a remote outback station. The nearly exclusively male cast brought a realistic physicality, masculinity and camaraderie to the shearing scenes—in contrast with the loneliness, isolation and alcoholism they experienced when not working.

UNKNOWN ARTIST, Sunday Too Far Away *daybill*, 1975

Courtesy the National Film and Sound Archive, copyright South Australian Film Corporation

"PICNIC AT HANGING ROCK"

1 EXT. HANGING ROCK. DAY 1

SOUND

PRACTICALLY NOTHING, EXCEPT PERHAPS
A FAINT LIGHT WHISPER OF WIND -
BUT HARDLY THERE - JUST A ZEPHYR.

MIST. SUPER TITLE CARD.

~~A TITLE CARD~~

AN AERIAL SHOT OF THE PEAKS AND SLOPES AND CAVERNS OF HANGING ROCK, STANDING UP OUT OF THE SURROUNDING LANDSCAPE OF PADDOCKS AND BUSH. APPROACHING, DRIFTING, LIFTING AND DIPPING LIGHTLY AND FREELY AS IF CAUGHT MOMENTARILY ON THE AIR CURRENTS. A BIRD'S EYE VIEW: THE CAMERA IS A FALCON, HOVERING AND DRIFTING ACROSS THE MONOLITH.

WOMEN'S VOICE

ON ST VALENTINE'S DAY IN THE SUMMER OF 1900, ~~A PARTY~~

~~On a summer's day in the year 1900,~~
a party of school girls set out to
picnic at Hanging Rock in the State
of Victoria. SEVERAL MEMBERS OF THE PARTY WERE NEVER TO RETURN. TO THIS DAY THE DISAPPEARANCE REMAINS A MYSTERY.

~~DOWN, DOWN, GENTLY DOWN, EVER SO SLOWLY AND LIGHTLY; THROUGH THE TREES, DOWN ....~~

~~THE SHOT IS GROUNDED. ON AN OPEN AREA CLOSE TO THE SUMMIT.~~

~~WE ARE CLOSING IN. CLOSER AND CLOSER. SLOWLY, ALMOST IMPERCEPTIBLY .....~~

~~TO A CLOSE CLOSE-UP. INSECTS. THE ENORMOUS HEAD AND MANDIBLES OF A GREAT RED BULL-ANT.~~

FROM BEHIND COMES HANGING ROCK, STANDING UP OUT OF EARLY MORNING.

~~WOMEN'S VOICE~~

SUPER MAIN

~~Several members of the party were never to return.~~

'Miranda! ... Miranda! ... Miranda!'

Picnic at Hanging Rock ranks among the finest films of the 1970s Australian New Wave. The haunting mystery, produced by Patricia Lovell and directed by Peter Weir, was a critical and commercial success around the world. Based on Joan Lindsay's 1967 novel of the same name, the film tells the story of four schoolgirls—including the ethereal Miranda (Anne-Louise Lambert)—who go missing during an excursion to Ngannelong (Hanging Rock), Victoria, on Valentine's Day 1900. It is perhaps best known for the eerie pan flute music of Romanian maestro Gheorghe Zamfir and for its unconventional ending.

CLIFF GREEN (1934–2020), *Screenplay for* Picnic at Hanging Rock, c. 1974

M.A.P.S. LITHOGRAPHY (1967–2009), *Picnic at Hanging Rock*, 1975

Courtesy the National Film and Sound Archive, Copyright Picnic Productions

Magazines

The 1970s were an exciting time for Australian magazine culture. Large circulation magazines were a mainstay of popular culture. Titles such as *Australian Women's Weekly* and *TV Week* were found in many Australian households. There were also counterculture magazines and specials such as *RAM* and *Tracks*.

Surfing pig

Captain Goodvibes was a cartoon strip about the adventures of a surfing pig, which appeared in the Australian surfing magazine *Tracks*. The Goodvibes compilations were also published as comic books and the character was also featured in a short animated film titled *Hot to Trot* (1977) and in a Double Jay radio serial.

TONY EDWARDS (b. 1944), *Captain Goodvibes: The Whole Earth Pigalogue*, 1975

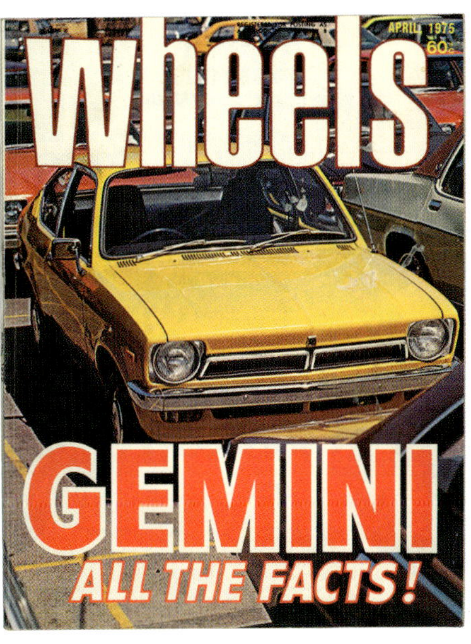

Cleo

Cleo was launched in 1972 under the leadership of inaugural editor Ita Buttrose. The magazine profiled successful women, explored women's health issues and provided sexual advice. It was also famous for featuring the first Australian nude male centrefold, starring actor Jack Thompson. *Cleo* ceased publication in 2016.

ITA BUTTROSE (editor, b. 1942),
Cleo, 1977

Wheels

Wheels magazine was one of a number of popular car magazines that celebrated Australian car culture. The annual announcement of Car of the Year was widely anticipated by readers.

PETER ROBINSON (editor, b. 1945),
Wheels, 1975

PHIL JARRETT (editor, b. 1951),
Tracks: The Surfers' Bible, 1975

ITA BUTTROSE (editor, b. 1942),
The Australian Women's Weekly, 1975

Heading overseas

In the early 1970s, Qantas purchased a fleet of Boeing 747 'Jumbo Jets' that reduced flight times to Britain and Europe, and opened up the possibility of travelling for a new generation. A European holiday quickly became the aspiration of many young people.

CON ASLANIS (active c. 1972–2006), *'Qantas want us.'*, c. 1975

QANTAS

Ask about their $420 Fading Blue Denim Flights To London.

WANT US.

Child's play

Outdoor play was common in the seventies. It was often child-led, unstructured and required imagination.

MERVYN BISHOP (b. 1945), *Children playing in the river, Mumeka, Arnhem Land, Northern Territory*, 1975

The growing demand for childcare

As increasing numbers of women moved into the workforce, women's organisations pushed governments for more childcare places and preschools. However, it took more than a decade for long day care and preschools to catch up with demand.

WOLFGANG SIEVERS (1913–2007), *Children on a swing at Tom Price, Western Australia*, 1975

Sounds of school

Screechy, shrill or melodious? From the 1950s onwards, many Australian children learnt the recorder in primary school. Playing an instrument develops coordination, fine motor skills, melody, pitch, breathing techniques and much more. Children in remote parts of Australia used shortwave radio to participate in School of the Air lessons for an hour each day. Either the Royal Flying Doctor Service or Australia Post was used to send their schoolwork back and forth to their teachers.

BRUCE HOWARD (b. 1936), *Jane Hopkins and her daughter, Peta, participating in School of the Air, Timber Creek, Northern Territory*, c. 1975

ALEX OZOLINS, *A recorder session with third-grade students, Northmead Primary School, Sydney*, 1975

Dancing in the diaspora

Dance is an avenue for storytelling, self-expression and honouring one's heritage in the diaspora. In 1975 Melbourne ranked as the world's fourth most populous 'Greek' city. Today, it is home to the largest population of Greek people living outside of Greece.

UNKNOWN PHOTOGRAPHER, *Members of 'The Bridge Theatre' group rehearse a Greek dance on the banks of Melbourne's Yarra River*, 1975

Let's dance

The National Black Theatre (NBT) operated between 1972 and 1977 in Redfern, Sydney, and provided a range of performing arts workshops and programs led by and for Indigenous Australians. The NBT emerged out of Indigenous activism and provided a platform for cultural expression. The Black Theatre Arts and Cultural Centre was run by the NBT from 1974 to 1977 and included modern dance—taught here by African American dancer Carole Johnson—among its offerings.

BILL PAYNE, *Carole Johnson leads a class in modern dance at the Black Theatre Arts and Cultural Centre, Sydney, 1975*

Welcome to Maria's Cafe

In 1963, Maria Otranto, aged just 17, left her village of Maddaloni, near Naples, Italy, for Geraldton, Western Australia. She worked in a cafe there for seven years before raising $16,500 to buy the business. Between 1946 and 1976 around 360,000 Italians migrated to Australia. Of these, 40,000 settled in Western Australia. During this period, around three-quarters of all Italian migrants came from southern Italy, specifically Sicily, Calabria, Abruzzo and Molise.

BRUCE HOWARD (b. 1936), *Maria's Cafe, Geraldton, Western Australia*, c. 1975

Meet at the mall

By the 1970s shopping malls had become the centre of suburban life in many Australian cities. Drawing business away from the traditional high street, the new centres functioned not only as a place to shop, but also as venues for performances and as places for teenagers to hang out.

WOLFGANG SIEVERS (1913–2007), *Public event and concert inside Highpoint Shopping Centre, Maribyrnong, Victoria, 1975*

White boots

St George fullback Graeme Langlands attracted criticism in the 1975 NSWRL Grand Final when, as part of a sponsorship deal he had with Adidas, he wore white boots instead of the traditional black. For many traditional rugby league fans, this nonconventional footwear invited bad luck. In what would be Langlands' last first-grade game, St George was defeated by Eastern Suburbs 38–0.

ROBERT PEARCE (*SYDNEY MORNING HERALD*) (b. 1949), *Graeme Langlands*, 1975

Courtesy Fairfax Media

Dennis Lillee

Lillee was one of the dominant Australian sports personalities of the 1970s. In 1975 he won home and away Ashes series. His partnerships with fellow paceman Jeff Thomson were particularly lethal. Together they claimed 95 wickets across the two series, shattering the will—and the bones—of their English opponents.

UNKNOWN PHOTOGRAPHER, *Dennis Lillee, fast bowler*, 1975

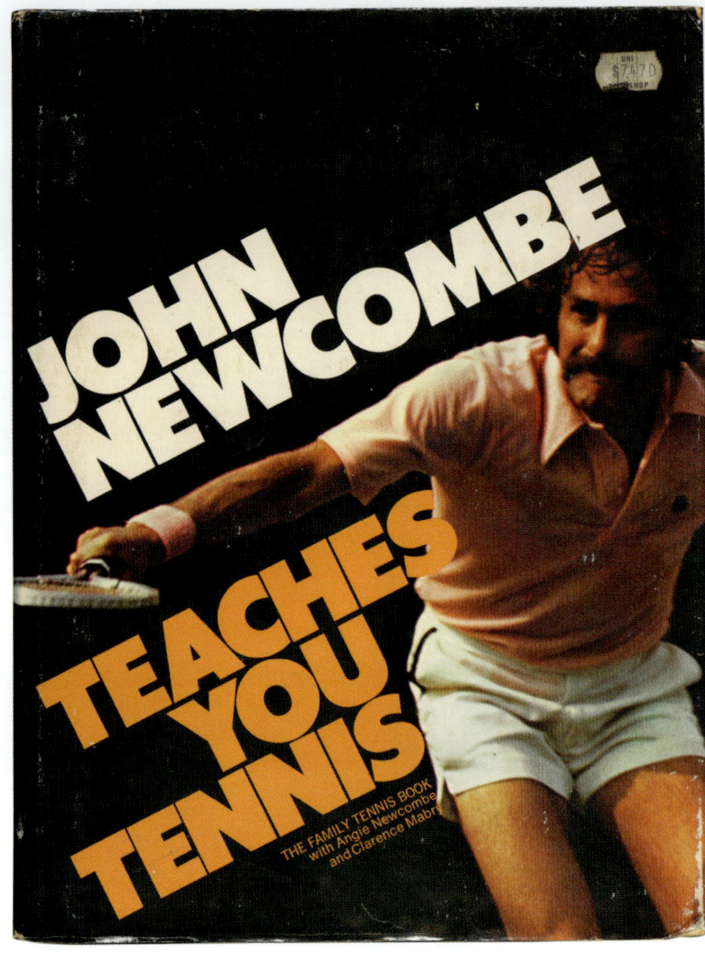

A year to remember

1975 was the last year that both the women's and men's singles championships at the Australian Tennis Open were won by Australians. Champions Evonne Goolagong and John Newcombe both released books that year. *Evonne!: On the Move* was an autobiography, while *John Newcombe Teaches You Tennis* was a coaching manual aimed at families.

EVONNE CAWLEY (b. 1951); BUD COLLINS (1929–2016), *Evonne!: On the Move*, 1975

JOHN NEWCOMBE (b. 1944); ANGIE NEWCOMBE (b. c. 1941); CLARENCE MABRY (1925–2013), *John Newcombe Teaches You Tennis: The Family Tennis Book*, 1975

Mining boom

From the 1960s Australia experienced a mining boom. The Mount Tom Price Mine was established in the Pilbara region of Western Australia in 1966. Export prices for Australian iron ore and coal rose steeply in the early 1970s, helping to fuel the mining boom. However, foreign ownership of mining companies generated considerable public debate.

WOLFGANG SIEVERS (1913–2007), *Hamersley Iron stockpiling iron ore for export, Dampier, Western Australia, 1975*

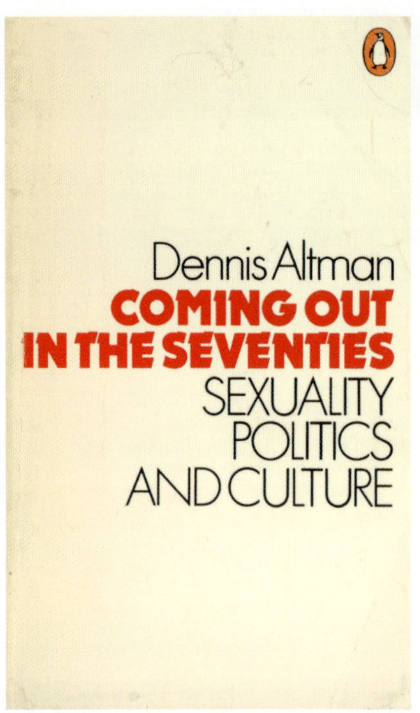

Writing in the seventies

Australian literature in the 1970s bore witness to changing ideas of Australian identity and nationhood. *The Rainbow Serpent*, an iconic picture book about the Rainbow Serpent Dreaming created by Lardil man Dick (Goobalathaldin) Roughsey and his friend Percy Trezise, was published in 1975. Contemporary classics set in suburbia emerged, such as *The Glass Canoe* (1976) by David Ireland and *Monkey Grip* (1977) by Helen Garner. Indigenous activist Charles Perkins, writer Antigone Kefala and others shared different perspectives—including First Nations and migrant experiences—through their writing.

DENNIS ALTMAN (b. 1943), *Coming Out in the Seventies*, 1979

ANTIGONE KEFALA (1931–2022), *The First Journey*, 1975

DAVID IRELAND (1927–2022), *The Glass Canoe*, 1976

HELEN GARNER (b. 1942), *Monkey Grip*, 1977

DON EDWARDS, *Percy Trezise and Dick Roughsey discuss a painting of the Rainbow Serpent with Prime Minister Gough Whitlam, 1975*

A treasured picture book

Lardil Elder Dick (Goobalathaldin) Roughsey and Percy Trezise's *The Rainbow Serpent* (1975) was the first Dreaming story to be published for a wide readership. The Rainbow Serpent appears in the creation stories of many Indigenous groups, each of which offers a different account of him and refers to him by a different name. This book refers to him as Goorialla and describes how he created the landscape of the Cape York Peninsula (which has many Aboriginal names), and how people transformed themselves into birds and animals to escape him. Trezise was a painter and writer who supported Roughsey's work and who collaborated with him on many children's books based on the Dreaming.

NEWS OF THE DAY

In January 1975 Australians watched the intense media coverage of Cyclone Tracy's devastating impact on Darwin after it had torn through the city in the early hours of the Christmas Day just past. Sixty-six people were killed, and over 80 per cent of the city's housing was destroyed.

On 5 January the bulk carrier *Lake Illawarra* collided with the Tasman Bridge in Hobart, collapsing a span of the bridge and killing 12 people. On 30 April North Vietnamese troops took control of South Vietnam's capital, Saigon, ending the Vietnam War. Fighting continued to rage elsewhere, however, with conflicts in South East Asia, Angola, Mozambique and East Timor (Timor-Leste).

Cyclone Tracy

At about midnight on Christmas Eve 1974 Cyclone Tracy hit Darwin. Hundreds of people were injured and 66 died. Only about 500 homes out of some 12,000 in the city remained habitable. Prime Minister Gough Whitlam flew into Darwin on 28 December. After touring the devastation, he said it was clear that many of the city's buildings erected after a cyclone in 1937 were unsuitable for the cyclone belt.

BRUCE HOWARD (b. 1936), *Prime Minister Gough Whitlam is taken on a tour of the wreckage in Darwin, 1974*

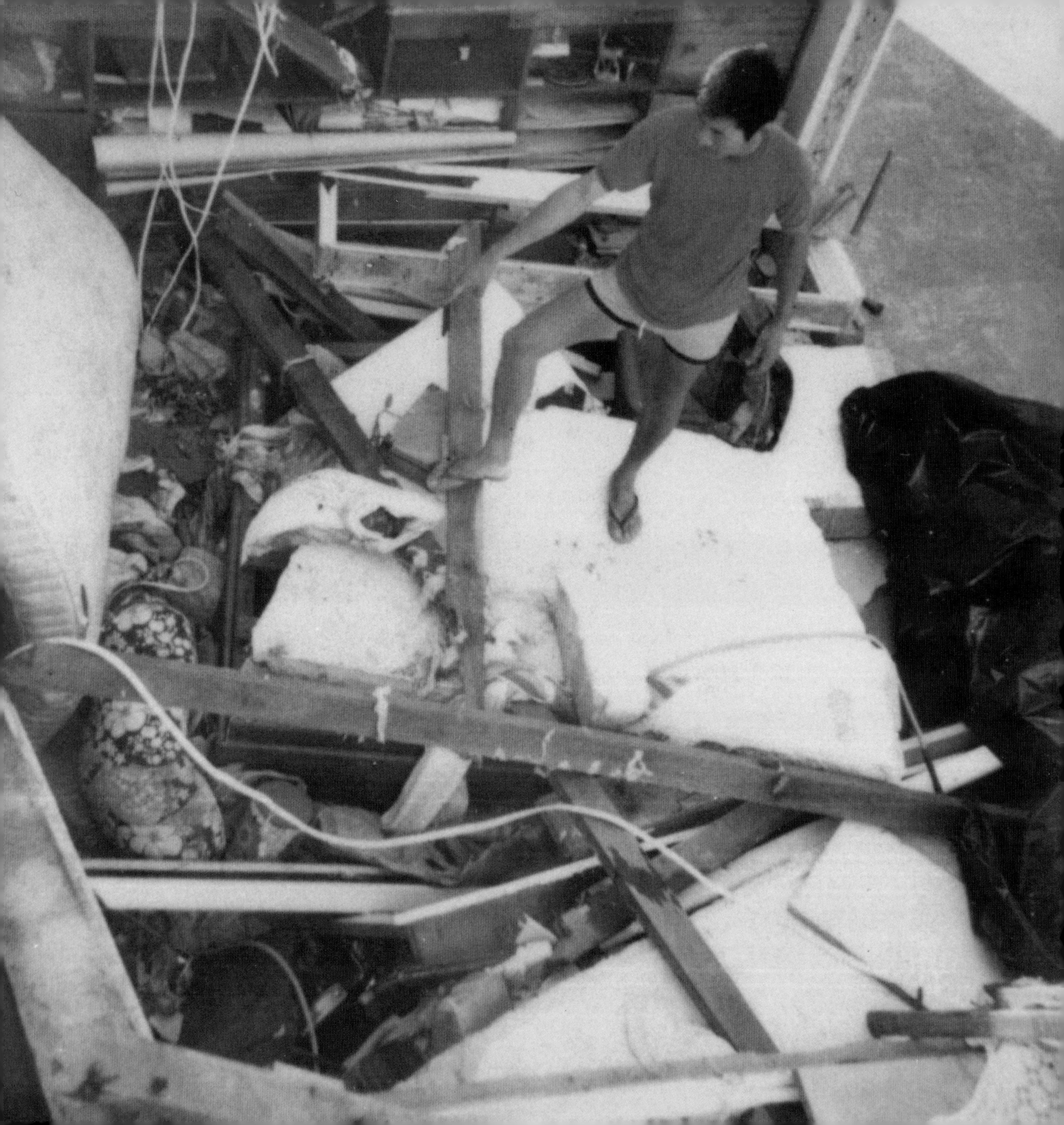

After the cyclone

'The plans had to be redrawn for the house. They had to be approved by the authorities as cyclone-proof. Things didn't move very fast in those days.'

William and Darwina Fong were home with four of their five children when Cyclone Tracy blew their house apart. Darwina and her 12-year-old daughter, Bonnie, whose pelvis had been broken, were evacuated to hospital in Sydney. Eldest daughter Sandra and her husband took care of the rest of the family. As they recovered, William bought a caravan for the family to live in for 18 months while they waited for their new home to be approved and built.

WILLIAM FONG, *Desmond Fong, age 16, in the remains of the bedroom where Darwina and Bonnie sheltered shortly before the roof collapsed*, 1975

UNKNOWN PHOTOGRAPHER, *William Fong repairing the family home*, 1975

WILLIAM FONG, *Restored Fong family home, Fannie Bay*, 1976

Images courtesy Darwina & William Fong Collection; Picture NT

Bridge collapse

On 5 January 1975 the bulk carrier *Lake Illawarra* collided with the Tasman Bridge in Hobart, collapsing its central span. Five cars plummeted into the Derwent River and the *Lake Illawarra* sank within minutes of the accident.

UNKNOWN PHOTOGRAPHER, *The Tasman Bridge in the aftermath of the collision of SS* Lake Illawarra *with its pylons,* 1975

Courtesy the National Archives of Australia

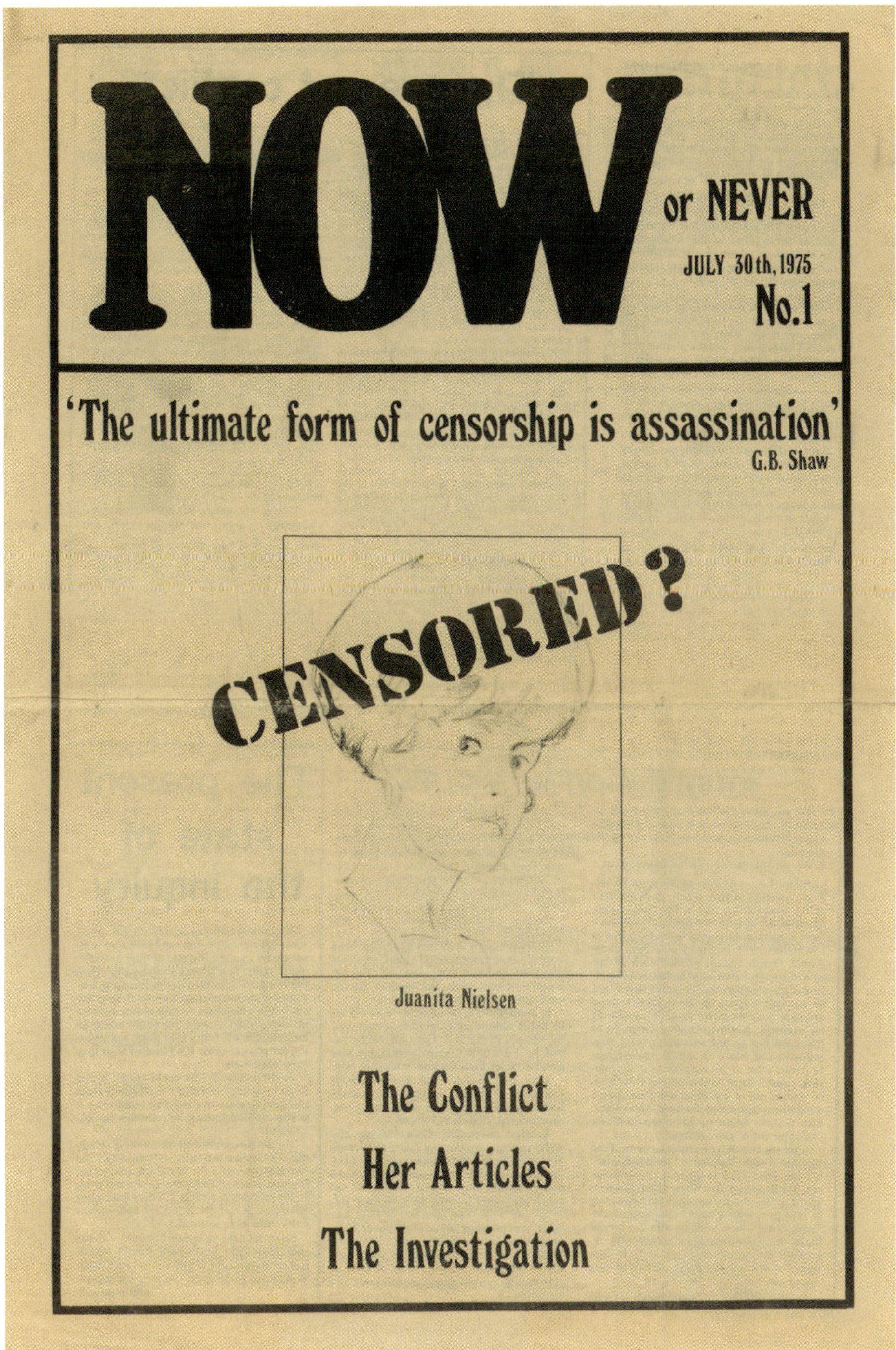

NOW or NEVER

JULY 30th, 1975

No.1

'The ultimate form of censorship is assassination'

G.B. Shaw

CENSORED?

Juanita Nielsen

The Conflict

Her Articles

The Investigation

An unsolved disappearance

Juanita Nielsen published the local Kings Cross newspaper *Now* in the early 1970s. She campaigned against the redevelopment of Victoria Street and successfully lobbied the Builders Labourers Federation (BLF) to impose a 'green ban' on the development. Nielsen disappeared in suspicious circumstances on 4 July 1975. A coronial inquest in 1983 found that she had been murdered, but did not identify either the perpetrators or the location of her body.

S. DE MERCI, *'Now or Never'*, 1975

Celebrating culture and community

The National Aborigines Day Observance Committee, or NADOC (the forerunner of NAIDOC), became a week-long event in 1975 with the theme 'Justice for Urban Aboriginal Children'. Previously held on the anniversary of the 1938 Day of Mourning, Aborigines Day was moved to the first Sunday in July to promote and celebrate the history, culture and achievements of Aboriginal and Torres Strait Islander peoples.

Murawina ('black woman') was a Redfern-based breakfast program that became a childcare centre and women's hostel in 1973. The centre was established and led by Aboriginal and Torres Strait Islander women, including founding members Aunty Norma Ingram and Aunty Millie Ingram. Their philosophy was to prepare children for the schooling system and to instil pride in their heritage.

UNKNOWN ARTIST, *Just This?—Or Justice? National Aborigines Week*, 1975

JUST THIS?
—OR JUSTICE

MURAWINA

ABORIGINAL PRE-SCHOOL Sydney NSW

NATIONAL ABORIGINES WEEK
7—13 JULY 1975

NATIONAL ABORIGINES DAY OBSERVANCE COMMITTEE

A new flag

Prior to gaining independence, Papua New Guinea had been subject to colonial rule by Britain and Germany. In 1884, the German empire claimed the north-east quarter of the island to exploit native labour for copra and cocoa plantations. The southern half of the east side of the island of New Guinea, later known as Papua, was annexed by Britain in 1888. Australian administration of Papua began in 1906 and was then extended to German New Guinea after the First World War. Papua New Guinea achieved independence on 16 September 1975.

UNKNOWN ARTIST, *Independence 1975: Our Flag—Our Country—Our People*, 1975

Courtesy Bill & Jan Gammage

TERENCE SPENCER (1917–2002);
MARGARET SPENCER (1916–2010),
Independence Day celebration at Port Moresby, Papua New Guinea, 1975

AUSTRALIA'S GREATEST FAMILY PAPER

BIGGEST SALE OF ANY PAPER IN AUSTRALIA

The Sun-Herald

FINAL

Incorporating "The Sunday Sun and Guardian" (No. 3747) and "The Sunday Herald" (No. 1360)

SUNDAY, APRIL 6, 1975

80 Pages including supplement.

FIFTEEN CENTS*

VIP treatment for a tiny passenger

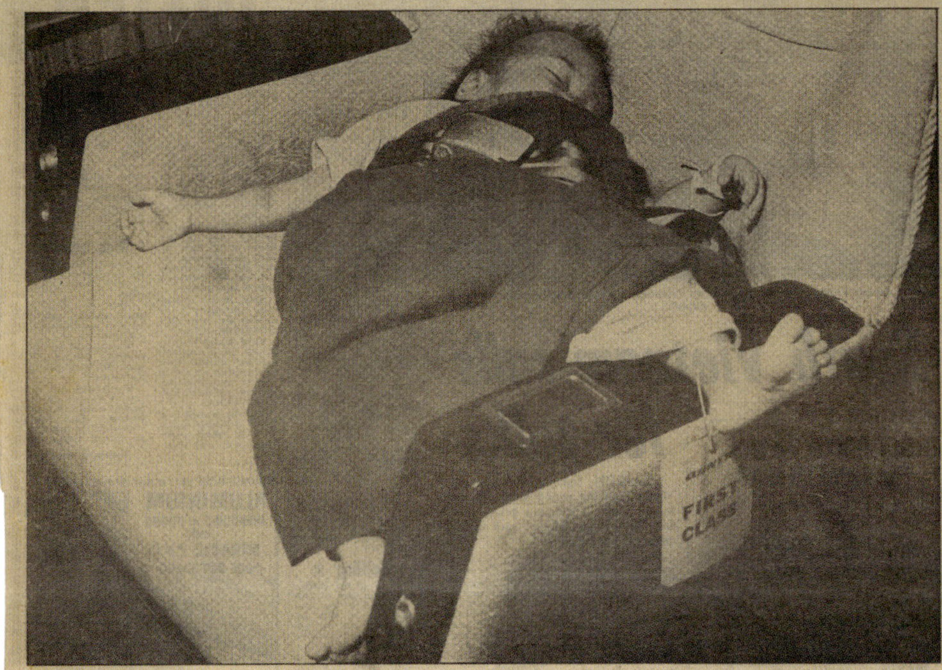

The first class label tells rescue officials that this tiny war orphan flown in from Bankok yesterday is among the seriously ill. Picture by Qantas photographer Barry Cullen. More pictures on pages 2, 3 and 4.

VIETNAM WAIFS FLY IN

By BOB CAMERON and MAURICE DUNLEVY

The first baby-lift of Vietnamese war orphans winged into Sydney yesterday — to one of the most emotional welcomes seen at the airport.

Women wept at the heartbreaking procession as 215 war waifs, some in makeshift cots made of cardboard boxes, were carried from a Qantas jumbo jet.

Ninety of them were immediately taken to hospital.

Captain Bert Smithwell, a Qantas pilot for 26 years, told reporters: "It was probably the saddest flight I have ever had to make. It was sad, it was very sad."

Most of the war orphans were red-eyed after their exhaustive nine-hour flight out of a war-torn Indo-China. But some still managed to wave and smile.

Pauline Lough, a Qantas ground hostess, burst into tears when she entered the aircraft.

• Continued on Page 2

WEATHER: (City) SW to S change. Few showers. Temp: 19 to 24 deg. (Details, map, page 23)

THE VIETNAMESE PEOPLE HAVE WON

CELEBRATE TONIGHT
City Square 5pm.

"Viet Namese Premier Nguyen Phan Long promised today to defeat what the French say are Communist-led Nationalists in six months if his government got United States military and economic aid".

New York Times,
February 15, 1950

"I can safely say that the end of the war is in sight".

General Paul D. Harkins
United States Commander, South Vietnam
Tokyo, Japan, October 31, 1963

"It can be said now that the defeat of the Communist forces in South Vietnam is inevitable. The only question is, how soon?

Richard M. Nixon,
Former Vice-President of the United States
Saigon, South Vietnam, April 17, 1967

"We finally have in sight the just peace we are seeking".

Richard M. Nixon
President of the United States
San Clemente, California, April 20, 1970

READ LETTER ON SOCIAL WORK PAGE 2

P.15 — WHAT DO YOU THINK OF I.S.S. NOW.

Operation Babylift

This was the name given to the mass evacuation of about 3,000 children from South Vietnam to many countries, including Australia. The first plane bound for the United States crashed 12 minutes after take-off, killing 143 babies and volunteers, including two Australians: Margaret Moses and Lee Makk. The children transported from Vietnam to Australia were given to families that were already approved for overseas adoptions.

THE SUN-HERALD, 'Vietnam Waifs Fly In', 1975

Fall of Saigon

On 30 April 1975, North Vietnamese Army tanks burst through the gate of the Presidential Palace in Saigon (now Ho Chi Minh City), ending the Vietnam War. The conflict in Vietnam, Laos and Cambodia was in effect a major proxy war, in which both the Soviet Union and China supported North Vietnam, and the United States, with its non-Communist allies, including Australia, supported South Vietnam.

FARRAGO, 'The Vietnamese People Have Won', Friday 2 May 1975

From independence to invasion

Following Portugal's withdrawal from East Timor, a coalition was formed between the Revolutionary Front for an Independent East Timor (Fretilin) and the Timorese Democratic Union (UDT) in January 1975. The UDT staged a coup in August, resulting in a short but violent civil war. On 28 November a democratically elected Fretilin government declared independence for what was to be the Democratic Republic of Timor-Leste. Nine days later East Timor was occupied by the Indonesian military.

PENNY TWEEDIE (1940–2011), *Unidentified activist attending an address by José Ramos-Horta [who would later become president of Timor-Leste]*, c. 1975

PENNY TWEEDIE (1940–2011), *Portrait of unidentified Fretilin soldier*, c. 1975

.FRETILIN

Angolan independence

Local political organisations formed in the Portuguese colony of Angola in the 1950s to demand human and civil rights, as well as independence. A war against colonial rule started on 4 February 1961. Portugal's authoritarian government was overthrown by a military coup in April 1974. This enabled all of Portugal's colonies to become independent, which Angola did on 11 November 1975. However, civil war then engulfed the country until 2002.

UNKNOWN ARTIST, *Solidarity Angola*, c. 1970–75

Courtesy the National Gallery of Australia

Learn from the peasants

The Cultural Revolution, launched in the People's Republic of China by Mao Zedong in 1966, lasted until 1976. The aim was to preserve Chinese socialism by removing all remnants of capitalist and traditional elements in Chinese society, but it resulted in widespread violence and chaos in which between 500,000 and 2 million people died.

UNKNOWN ARTIST, 向贫下中农学习 为贫下中农服务 *[Learn from the Poor and Lower-Middle Peasants and Serve Them]*, 1975

WE ARE WOMEN

1975 was a pivotal year in the Second Wave feminist movement of the 1960s–70s. Many feminists banded together to advocate for women's rights and greater awareness of the barriers that held women back from achieving equality.

The United Nations recognised the growing power of 'women's liberation' by declaring 1975 to be International Women's Year. The aim was to end entrenched discrimination against women and enable them to participate more fully in economic, social and political life. International Women's Year was marked in Australia and provided a platform for some women to have a light shone on their experiences and aspirations. Since 1975, 8 March has been officially recognised as International Women's Day.

On the march

On 8 March 1975—International Women's Day—up to 5,000 people marched down Melbourne's streets to raise awareness of gender inequality in Australia. The march was preceded by an all-women play, performed at City Square, which depicted the sheer extent of the oppression suffered by women in the home.

JOHN MCKINNON, *Women carry placards at the International Women's Day march, Melbourne, 1975*

A safe space

The Elsie Women's Refuge Night Shelter opened in Glebe, Sydney, in 1974. It was Australia's first refuge for women and children fleeing domestic and family violence. It was established by Anne Summers and other activists, who occupied two abandoned houses. In addition to supplying crisis accommodation, the refuge offered support and advice and was notable for the feminist outlook those who worked there brought to the provision of essential services for women in need.

UNKNOWN PHOTOGRAPHER, *Staff assisting women seeking refuge at the Elsie Women's Shelter, Sydney, 1975*

ANNE SUMMERS

DAMNED WHORES AND GOD'S POLICE

The Colonization of Women in Australia

A history of Australian women

Damned Whores and God's Police: The Colonization of Women in Australia, a landmark publication by historian and journalist Dr Anne Summers, was published in 1975. The book unpacks the stereotypes through which women had been framed—notably the dichotomy of the 'damned whore' and the 'virtuous, pious' woman.

ANNE SUMMERS (b. 1945), *Damned Whores and God's Police: The Colonization of Women in Australia*

Ringwood, Vic.: Penguin Books, 1975

Equal opportunity

Second Wave feminism brought legislative change that made it illegal to pay a woman less for doing the same job as a man. This helped challenge traditional gender roles in the workplace, including apprenticeship programs. At a time when women were under-represented in certain industries, this advertising scheme provided employment opportunities for young women.

PUBLIC SERVICE COMMISSION, *Who Says Girls Can't Be Apprentices Too?*, c. 1970–75

Advising the PM on women's affairs

In 1973 Elizabeth Reid, a philosophy tutor at the Australian National University, became the first person to be appointed to an official role as women's affairs advisor to an Australian prime minister. Reid worked with Gough Whitlam's Labor government in a key role that involved advising on—and raising the profile of—women's affairs. This included in the international arena, such as the Commonwealth Heads of Government meeting in Jamaica in 1975.

Identification card for Elizabeth Reid to attend the Commonwealth Heads of Government meeting, Jamaica, 1975

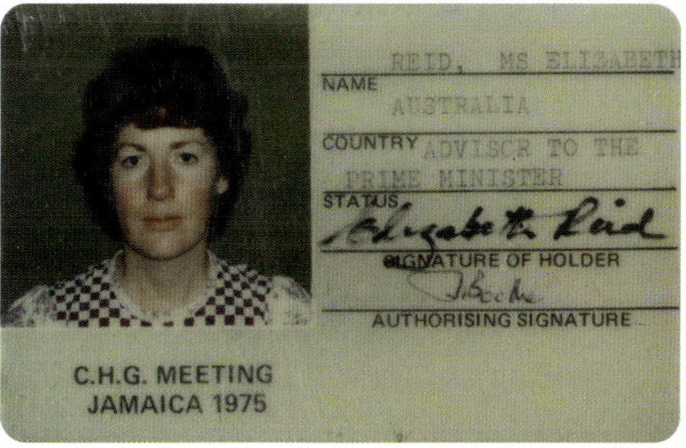

In the PM's ear

Elizabeth Reid chaired the National Advisory Committee on International Women's Year. The Committee organised a range of activities, including the Women in Politics conference, held in Canberra towards the end of the year, and the Australian delegation to the international Mexico conference. Reid resigned from her position in late 1975, following the decision to move her role out of the Office of the Prime Minister.

MALCOLM LINDSAY, *Mr Whitlam discusses International Women's Year with members of the National Advisory Committee, Ms Elizabeth Reid and Mr James Oswin, 1974*

MEETING IN MEXICO

WORLD CONFERENCE OF THE INTERNATIONAL WOMEN'S YEAR, 1975

Faces at IWY.

United Nations

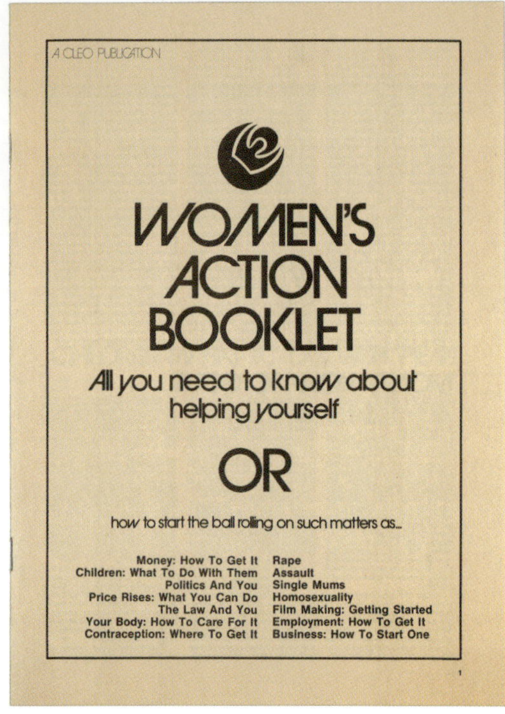
A CLEO PUBLICATION

WOMEN'S ACTION BOOKLET

All you need to know about helping yourself

OR

how to start the ball rolling on such matters as...

Money: How To Get It
Children: What To Do With Them
Politics And You
Price Rises: What You Can Do
The Law And You
Your Body: How To Care For It
Contraception: Where To Get It
Rape
Assault
Single Mums
Homosexuality
Film Making: Getting Started
Employment: How To Get It
Business: How To Start One

1

Women of the world

The UN Conference on Women, a key plank of International Women's Year festivities, was held from 19 June to 2 July 1975 in Mexico. Representatives from across the world gathered to connect and to discuss women's affairs. Subsequent conferences on women followed, contributing to the creation of international benchmarks around women's issues.

Meeting in Mexico: The Story of the World Conference of the International Women's Year, 1975

Essential information

The *Women's Action Booklet*, published by *Cleo* magazine with the Australian Advisory Committee on International Women's Year, provided information and resources on a range of topics affecting women. Some of these issues were stigmatised at the time and resources were not widely accessible. The booklet includes the names and contact details of organisations where women could get assistance on matters such as sexual health, employment and childcare.

UNKNOWN AUTHOR, *Women's Action Booklet: All You Need to Know about Helping Yourself*, c. 1975

Women on the big screen

The International Women's Film Festival was held in various Australian cities in October 1975. Showcasing films by and about women, the festival emerged from activism around the lack of inclusion of women in the film industry and the barriers to screening women's films. It was supported by the Film and Television Board of the Australia Council and the Australian Committee for International Women's Year.

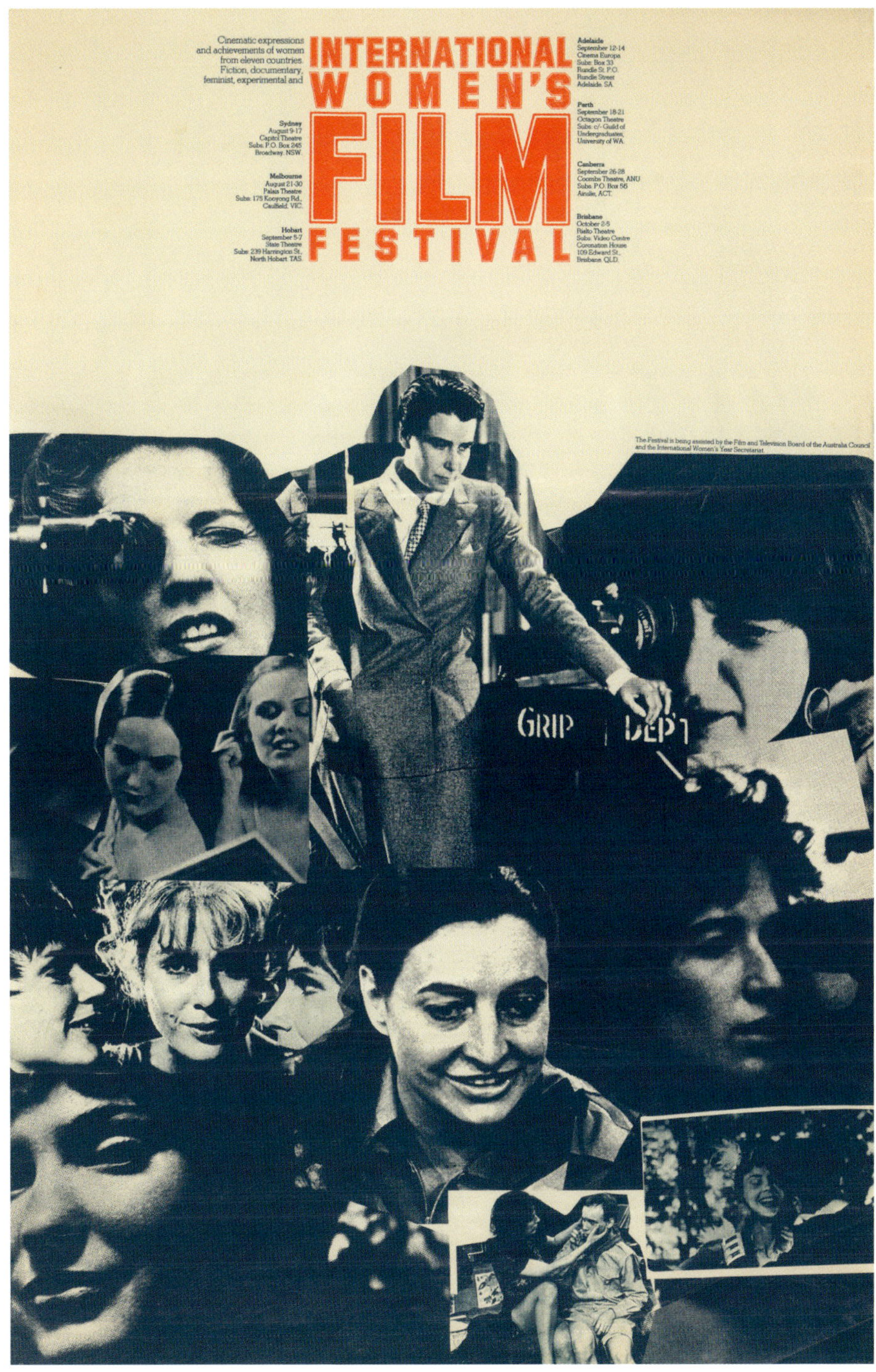

UNKNOWN ARTIST, *International Women's Film Festival*, 1975

CHANGING TIMES

The 1970s saw dramatic changes in Australian cultural and political life. After 23 years of conservative government, the Labor Party, which came to power in 1972 under the leadership of Gough Whitlam, began delivering an aggressive reform agenda. Policies implemented included abolishing tertiary education fees, reducing the voting age to 18, establishing universal healthcare and passing the *Racial Discrimination Act 1975*. Indigenous Australians were also pressuring the government to recognise land rights. The Whitlam government made supporting the arts a priority, and encouraged artists to tell Australian stories.

The female gaze

Vale Street is one of the most recognisable photographs in Australian art history. Carol Jerrems was just 26 when she captured this iconic image of a topless young woman flanked by two young men. The woman's commanding presence is reinforced by her central position and her confident, direct gaze. The ankh pendant she wears conveys a feminist message, this ancient Egyptian hieroglyphic symbol for 'life' having been embraced by Second Wave feminists. This test print of Vale Street is included in Jerrems' papers, which were recently acquired by the Library.

CAROL JERREMS (1949–1980), *Vale Street [test print]*, 1975

Evening In Byzantium

Power couple

Husband and wife Bob Ellis and Anne Brooksbank were both accomplished writers committed to telling Australian stories. In the mid-1970s they owned the Stables Theatre in Darlinghurst, the original home for the Nimrod Street Theatre and later the home for the Griffin Theatre Company.

ROBERT MCFARLANE (1942–2023), *Authors Bob Ellis and Anne Brooksbank at the Stables Theatre, Kings Cross, Sydney, 1976*

BRUCE HOWARD (b. 1936), *Judy Cassab, Bellevue Hill, New South Wales, c. 1975*

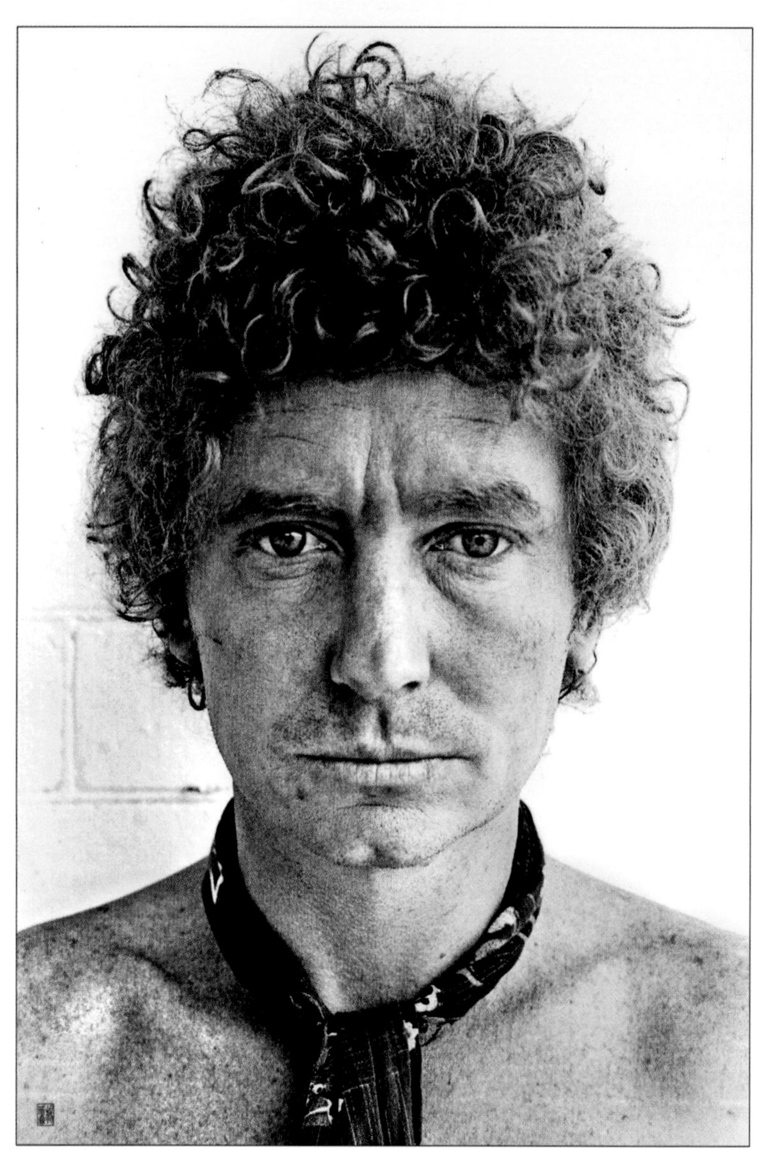

WILLIAM YANG (b. 1943), *Brett Whiteley*, 1975
My Generation series

AUSTRALIA
1976

A new honours system

The Order of Australia was instituted by Queen Elizabeth II on 14 February 1975, on the recommendation of the Whitlam government. It replaced the traditional Imperial honours system. The medals for the newly created honours were designed by Australian artist Stuart Devlin.

STUART DEVLIN (1931–2018), *Design for the Companion of the Order of Australia award*, c. 1975

Courtesy the Office of the Official Secretary to the Governor-General

Universal health care

Creating a national health insurance scheme was a central plank of the Labor Party's 1972 election campaign. The first attempts to establish the new scheme were blocked in the Senate in 1974. Following a double dissolution election—one in which all Senate and House of Representatives seats are contested at the same time—the legislation was passed by a joint sitting of parliament in August 1974. Medibank began on 1 July 1975.

DEPARTMENT OF SOCIAL SECURITY, *Medibank and You*, 1975

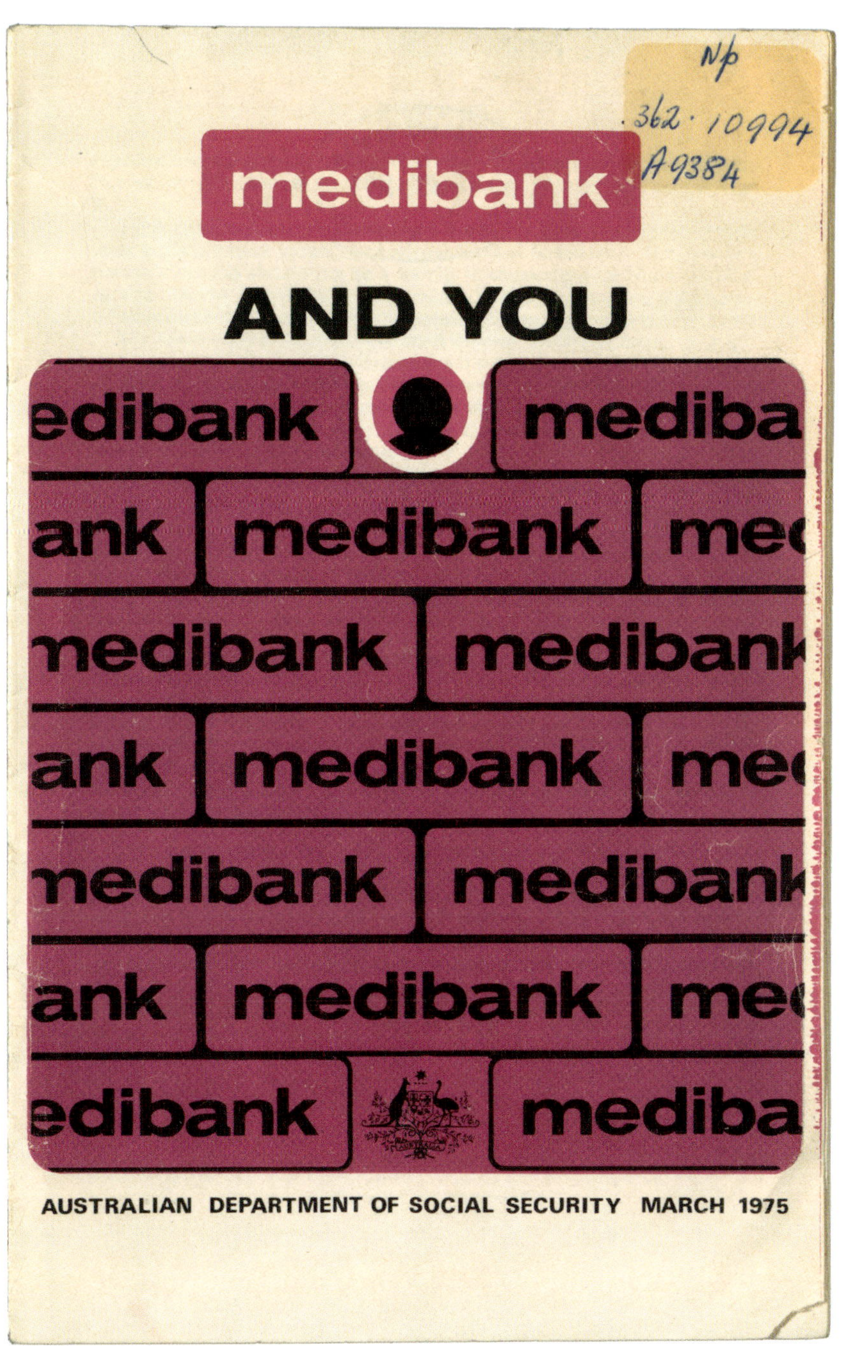

Protecting the reef

In 1974 Labor prime minister Gough Whitlam announced that his government would pass legislation to protect the Great Barrier Reef from oil drilling. The *Great Barrier Reef Marine Park Act* received royal assent on 20 June 1975.

G. FORSTER (b. 1949), *Visit the fabulous Hook Island underwater coral observatory on Australia's Great Barrier Reef*, c. 1960s

Gurindji

1975 also saw the culmination of the campaign for land rights for the Gurindji people at Daguragu (Wattie Creek) in the Northern Territory. What became known as the 'Wave Hill Walk-Off' began as a strike by Indigenous pastoral workers on Wave Hill Station for better pay and conditions in 1966 and evolved into a struggle for land rights that would dominate Australian politics for years to come.

UNKNOWN MAKER, *Gurindji campaign*, 1975

GURIND
CAMPAIG
PUBLIC MEETING
SPEAKERS:-
FRANK HARDY
SEN. KEEFFE

wattie creek now

"We don't want to be under the axe all the time."

8 PM

MON. 27TH MARCH
TEACHER'S FED
300 SUSSEX ST

Handback

On 16 August 1975 Indigenous photographer Mervyn Bishop captured the moment when Prime Minister Gough Whitlam poured a handful of red dirt into land rights activist Vincent Lingiari's hands at a ceremony at Daguragu (Wattie Creek), symbolising the return of the land to the Gurindji people.

MERVYN BISHOP (b. 1945), *Prime Minister Gough Whitlam pours soil into the hand of Gurindji Traditional Owner and land rights leader Vincent Lingiari at Daguragu [Wattie Creek], Northern Territory, 1975*

Land rights

The success of the Gurindji campaign played an important role in the broader campaign for Indigenous land rights. In 1976 the federal government passed the *Aboriginal Land Rights (Northern Territory) Act 1976*, the first legislation to provide a process by which Indigenous people could claim land rights for Country.

UNKNOWN ARTIST, *Real Land Rights or Political Gimmick? The Northern Territory Land Rights Bill*, c. 1975

THE DISMISSAL

As 1975 came to a close, voters were worried by rampant inflation and economic stagnation. After a series of controversies and ministerial sackings in 1974–75, the Opposition parties blocked the federal budget. The deadlock in the Senate was dramatically broken on 11 November, when Governor-General Sir John Kerr dismissed Whitlam's government and appointed Liberal leader Malcolm Fraser as caretaker prime minister. The federal election held soon afterwards confirmed the Coalition's hold on power.

Sacked

Sir John Kerr handed his letter of dismissal to Gough Whitlam at Government House in Yarralumla at 1pm on 11 November 1975. The news spread quickly, with headlines of the sacking on the front page of the afternoon newspapers as people emerged from work in the early evening.

ROBERT MCFARLANE (1942–2023), *Newspaper vendor holding a copy of the* Daily Mirror *with the headline 'Kerr sacks Gough!', Martin Place, Sydney, 1975*

'Well may we say ...'

Gough Whitlam looked on as David Smith, official secretary to the Governor-General, read the proclamation dissolving both houses of parliament. He then stepped forward to make one of the most famous speeches in Australian political history. 'Ladies and gentlemen,' he declared, 'well may we say "God Save the Queen" because nothing will save the Governor-General.'

UNKNOWN PHOTOGRAPHER,
The Governor-General's official secretary reads the proclamation dissolving parliament on the steps of Parliament House, Canberra, 1975

Caretaker PM

Following the 11 November dismissal of Whitlam, Malcolm Fraser, leader of the Liberal Party, was sworn in as a caretaker prime minister. In the federal election held on 13 December, the Coalition (comprising the Liberal Party and the Country Party, led by Doug Anthony) won the largest parliamentary majority achieved to that time in Australian history.

UNKNOWN PHOTOGRAPHER,
Malcolm Fraser at Parliament House, Canberra, 1975

Protest!

Demonstrations were held around Australia to protest the dismissal of the Whitlam government. Many argued that Kerr's dismissal of Whitlam had damaged Australian democracy. The governor-general's vice-regal morning dress, including the top hat, became a symbol of what many saw as the misuse of power.

RICK AMOR (b. 1948), *Nov. 11: Rally Treasury Gardens*, 1976

Courtesy the artist and Niagara Galleries, Melbourne

IMAGE CREDITS

Cover image:
John McKinnon
Women on the march wave their placards at the International Women's Day march, Melbourne, 1975
Courtesy the Australian Information Service
nla.obj-137045864

Internal images:

2
Unknown photographer
Gough Whitlam speaking on the steps of Parliament House, Parliament House, Canberra 1975
Courtesy the Australian Information Service
nla.obj-147274349

4
Greg Macainsh (b. 1950)
Ego Is Not a Dirty Word
St Leonards, NSW: Castle Music, 1975
nla.cat-vn1843249

6
Stewart McCrae (1919–2008)
'Can't you think of something except "It's sink or swim"?' c. 1972–1975
Stewart McCrae cartoon collection
nla.obj-145832435

8
Unknown photographer
Malcolm Fraser walking beside car at Parliament House, Canberra 1975
Courtesy the Australian Information Service
nla.obj-147275242

10
Unknown photographer
Heather McKay playing a forehand drive during a squash match in Canberra 1972
Courtesy the Australian Information Service
nla.obj-137403541

13
Alex Stitt (1937–2016)
Life. Be in it.
Canberra: Australian Government Publishing Service, 1977
nla.cat-vn7124960

14 (left)
Bon Scott (1946–1980);
Malcolm Young (1953–2017);
Angus Young (b. 1955)
High Voltage
Sydney: J Albert & Son, 1975
nla.cat-vn48380

14 (right top)
John Rostill (1942–1973)
If You Love Me (Let Me Know), performed by Olivia Newton-John
Pyrmont, NSW: Festival Music, 1974
nla.cat-vn1864626

14 (right bottom)
Freddie Mercury (1946–1991)
Bohemian Rhapsody
St. Leonards, NSW: Castle Music, c. 1975
nla.cat-vn3208136

15
Benny Andersson (b. 1946);
Stig Anderson (1931–1997);
Björn Ulvaeus (b. 1945)
Mamma Mia
Milsons Point, NSW: Ivan Mogull Music, c. 1975
nla.cat-vn2736038

16
Unknown photographer
Sherbet
Melbourne: Brownhall Printing, c. 1976
nla.obj-138085916

17
Peter Kelly
Marcia Hines with Australia's Daly-Wilson Big Band on international tour 1975
Courtesy the Australian Information Service
nla.obj-136981914

18
Kamahl: 1975 Australian Tour
Camini Promotions, 1975
nla.cat-vn3528914

19
Unknown artist
Double Jay Rock '1540' 1978
Courtesy The National Film and Sound Archive

20
Rennie Ellis (1940–2003)
Ian 'Molly' Meldrum, Prahran 1978
nla.obj-145149344

21
Neil Curtis (album art, 1950–2006);
Skyhooks: Graeme 'Shirley' Strachan (1952–2001);
Greg Macainsh (b. 1950);
Red Symons (b. 1949);
Bob Starkie (b. c. 1953);
Imants 'Freddie' Strauks (b. 1950)
Ego Is Not a Dirty Word 1975

22
Grahame Bond (b. 1943)
Farewell Aunty Jack
Hunters Hill, NSW: Picture Record Publishing, c. 1974
nla.cat-vn2610240

23
Colour TV: What to Look for When Buying a Set
Chippendale, NSW: Australian Consumers' Association, 1977
nla.cat-vn1285282

24
Frank Cook (editor)
TV Week
Melbourne: Southdown Press, 1975

25
Swami Sarasvati (c. 1941–2023)
Enjoy Living through Yoga
Kenthurst, NSW: Sarasvati International, 1975
nla.cat-vn2186722

26
Unknown photographer
Tom Baker as Doctor Who c. 1974–81
RGR Collection / Alamy Stock Photo

27
Bruce Postle (b. 1940)
Norman Gunston and Denise Drysdale at the Logie Awards presentation night, each with their Gold Logie 1976
nla.obj-148394048

28
Margaret Fulton (1924–2019)
The Margaret Fulton Crock-Pot Cookbook
Sydney: Summit books, 1976
nla.cat-vn2834240

29 (top left)
Diana Wynne (editor)
When the Boss Comes to Dinner
Sydney: Australian Home Journal, c. 1975
nla.cat-vn366880

29 (top middle)
Babette Hayes (b. 1938)
Party Fare
Melbourne: Nelson, 1970
nla.cat-vn1365283

29 (top right)
South Australian Country Women's Association
Calendar of Meat and Fish Recipes in Metric: One for Every Day of the Year
Adelaide: The Association, 1975
nla.cat-vn2088712

29 (bottom left)
Bernard King (1934–2002)
Bernard King's Spring Cookbook
Adelaide: Rigby, 1977
nla.cat-vn2785443

29 (bottom right)
Recipes 1975
Kogarah, NSW: St George County Council, 1975
nla.cat-vn1816748

30
Bruce Howard (b. 1936)
Ruth Tarvydas, Perth, Western Australia c. 1975
nla.obj-147730529

31
A flair for flares
Colonials have a flair for the leggy look: easy living long lasting jeans
Melbourne: Sterling Clothing, c. 1970–75
nla.obj-626480664

33
Unknown artist
Sunday Too Far Away *daybill* 1975
Courtesy The National Film and Sound Archive

34
Cliff Green (1934–2020)
Screenplay for Picnic at Hanging Rock c. 1974
Papers of Cliff Green c. 1960–1988
nla.obj-243071929
Courtesy the Estate of Cliff Green and Picnic Productions

35
M.A.P.S. Lithography (1967–2009)
Picnic at Hanging Rock 1975
Courtesy The National Film and Sound Archive

36
Tony Edwards (b. 1944)
Captain Goodvibes: The Whole Earth Pigalogue
Avalon Beach, NSW: Tracks Publishing Co., 1975
nla.cat-vn6290005

37 (top left)
Pat Dasey (editor)
Cleo
Sydney: Australian Consolidated Press, November 1975

37 (top right)
Peter Robinson (editor, b. 1945)
Wheels
Sydney: Murray Publishers, 1975

37 (bottom left)
Phil Jarratt (editor)
Tracks: The Surfers' Bible
Avalon Beach, NSW: Tracks Publishing Co., 1975
nla.cat-vn2257741

37 (bottom right)
Ita Buttrose (editor, b. 1942)
The Australian Women's Weekly
Sydney: Are Media Pty Ltd, 19 February 1975
nla.cat-vn1935438

38–39
Con Aslanis (active c. 1972–2006)
'Qantas want us.'
Sydney: Qantas, c. 1975
nla.obj-2825910466

40 (top)
Mervyn Bishop (b. 1945)
Children playing in the river, Mumeka, Arnhem Land, Northern Territory 1975
Mervyn Bishop collection of photographs, 1963–89
nla.obj-153510324
Courtesy Mervyn Bishop and Josef Lebovic Gallery, Sydney

40 (bottom)
Wolfgang Sievers (1913–2007)
Teacher and small children in a classroom at Tom Price, Western Australia 1975
Wolfgang Sievers Photographic Archive
nla.obj-160837526

41 (top)
Bruce Howard (b. 1936)
Jane Hopkins and her daughter, Peta, participating in School of the Air, Timber Creek, Northern Territory c. 1975
nla.obj-147735965

41 (bottom)
Alex Ozolins
A recorder session with third-grade students, Northmead Primary School, Sydney 1975
Courtesy the Australian Information Service
nla.obj-136979455

42
Unknown photographer
Members of 'The Bridge Theatre' group rehearse a Greek dance on the banks of Melbourne's Yarra River 1975
nla.obj-136808598

43
Bill Payne
Carole Johnson leads a class in modern dance at the Black Theatre Arts and Cultural Centre, Sydney 1975
Courtesy the Australian Information Service
nla.obj-138165005

44
Bruce Howard (b. 1936)
Maria's Cafe, Geraldton, Western Australia c. 1975
nla.obj-147718610

45
Wolfgang Sievers (1913–2007)
Public event and concert inside Highpoint Shopping Centre, Maribyrnong, Victoria 1975
Wolfgang Sievers Photographic Archive
nla.obj-161102811

46
Robert Pearce (b. 1949)
Graeme Langlands 1975
Courtesy Fairfax Media

47
Australian Information Service photograph
Dennis Lillee, Fast Bowler 1975
nla.cat-vn3075746

48 (left)
Evonne Cawley (b. 1951);
Bud Collins (1929–2016)
Evonne!: On the Move
New York: Dutton, 1975
nla.cat-vn291466

48 (right)
John Newcombe (b. 1944);
Angie Newcombe (b. c. 1941);
Clarence Mabry (1925–2013)
John Newcombe Teaches You Tennis: The Family Tennis Book
New York: A Tennis Magazine Book, 1975

49
Wolfgang Sievers (1913–2007)
Hamersley Iron stockpiling iron ore for export, Dampier, Western Australia 1975
Wolfgang Sievers Photographic Archive
nla.obj-160338313

50 (top left)
Dennis Altman (b. 1943)
Coming Out in the Seventies
Sydney: Penguin Books, 1979
nla.cat-vn3706942

50 (top right)
Antigone Kefala (1931–2022)
The First Journey
Sydney: Wild and Woolley, 1975
nla.cat-vn672752

50 (bottom left)
David Ireland (1927–2022)
The Glass Canoe
Melbourne: Macmillan, 1976
nla.cat-vn685939

50 (bottom right)
Helen Garner (b. 1942)
Monkey Grip
Melbourne: McPhee Gribble Publishers, 1977
nla.cat-vn3564818

51
Don Edwards
Percy Trezise and Dick (Goobalathaldin) Roughsey discuss a painting of the Rainbow Serpent with Prime Minister Gough Whitlam 1975
Courtesy the Australian Information Service
nla.obj-138160481

53
Bruce Howard (b. 1936)
Prime Minister Gough Whitlam is taken on a tour of the wreckage in Darwin 1974
Bruce Howard collection of photographs for *Herald and Weekly Times*, Melbourne, 1955–1995
nla.obj-148158669

54
William Fong (1921–2001)
Desmond Fong, age 16, in the remains of the bedroom where Darwina and Bonnie sheltered shortly before the roof collapsed 1975
Top End Chinese collection
nla.cat-vn1414567
Top End Chinese collection: Images courtesy Darwina & William Fong Collection; Picture NT

55 (top)
Unknown photographer
William Fong repairing the family home 1975
Top End Chinese collection: Images courtesy Darwina & William Fong Collection; Picture NT
nla.cat-vn1414567

55 (bottom)
William Fong (1921–2001)
Restored home, Fannie Bay, Northern Territory, 1976
Top End Chinese collection: Images courtesy Darwina & William Fong Collection; Picture NT
nla.cat-vn1414567

56
Unknown photographer
The Tasman Bridge in the aftermath of the collision of SS Lake Illawarra *with its pylons* 1975
Courtesy the National Archives of Australia

57
S. De Merci
'Now or Never' 1975
Potts Point, NSW: A. King, 1975
nla.cat-vn920506

58
Unknown artist
Just This?—Or Justice: National Aborigines Week
Australia: National Aborigines Day Observance Committee, 1975
nla.obj-133513748

59
Unknown artist
Independence 1975: Our Flag—Our Country—Our People 1975
Courtesy Bill & Jan Gammage

60–61
Terence Spencer (1917–2002); Margaret Spencer (1916–2010)
Independence Day Celebrations, Port Moresby, Papua New Guinea 1975
nla.obj-145644669

62
The Sun-Herald
'Vietnam Waifs Fly In'
Sydney: John Fairfax, 1975
Papers of Elaine Moir, c. 1971–c. 1985
nla.cat-vn6159065

63
'The Vietnamese People Have Won'
Melbourne: Farrago, 2 May 1975
Papers of Elaine Moir, c. 1971–c. 1985
nla.cat-vn6159065

64
Penny Tweedie (1940–2011)
Unidentified activist attending an address by Jose Ramos-Horta [who would later become president of Timor-Leste] n.d.
Penny Tweedie archive, 1958–2010
nla.cat-vn6197605

65
Penny Tweedie (1940–2011)
Portrait of unidentified Fretilin soldier n.d.
Penny Tweedie archive, 1958–2010
nla.cat-vn6197605

66
Unknown artist
Solidarity Angola
Ithaca, New York: Glad Day Press, c. 1970–75
Courtesy the National Gallery of Australia

67
向贫下中农学习 为贫下中农服务
[Learn from the Poor and Lower-Middle Peasants and Serve Them]
Beijing: Renmin Tiyu Chubanshe, 1975
nla.obj-513615678

69
John McKinnon
Women carry placards at the International Women's Day march, Melbourne 1975
Courtesy the Australian Information Service
nla.obj-137045864

70
Unknown photographer
Staff assisting women seeking refuge at the Elsie Women's Shelter, Sydney 1975
Courtesy the Australian Information Service
nla.obj-661792766

71
Anne Summers (b. 1945)
Damned Whores and God's Police: The Colonization of Women in Australia
Ringwood, Vic.: Penguin Books, 1975
nla.cat-vn663055

72
Public Service Commission
Who Says Girls Can't Be Apprentices Too?
Australia: Public Service Commission, c. 1970–75
nla.obj-133715704

73 (top)
Malcolm Lindsay
Mr Whitlam discusses International Women's Year with members of the National Advisory Committee, Ms Elizabeth Reid and Mr James Oswin
1974
Courtesy the Australian Information Service
nla.obj-137047143

73 (bottom)
Identification card for Elizabeth Reid to attend the Commonwealth Heads of Government meeting, Jamaica 1975
Papers of Elizabeth Reid 1963–1981
nla.cat-vn2057202

74 (left)
Meeting in Mexico: The Story of the World Conference of the International Women's Year
New York: United Nations, 1975
nla.cat-vn100680

74 (right)
Women's Action Booklet: All You Need to Know about Helping Yourself
Sydney: Cleo, c. 1975
nla.cat-vn2775476

75
Unknown artist
International Women's Film Festival
Australia: The Film and Television Board of the Australia Council; International Women's Year Secretariat, 1975
nla.cat-vn1375236

77
Carol Jerrems (1949–1980)
Vale Street [test print] 1975
Papers of Carol Jerrems 1958–2010
nla.cat-vn10002960
Courtesy the Estate of Carol Jerrems

78
Robert Mcfarlane (1942–2023),
Authors Bob Ellis and Anne Brooksbank at the Stables Theatre, Kings Cross, Sydney 1976
nla.cat-vn6610930

79
Bruce Howard (b. 1936)
Judy Cassab, Bellevue Hill, New South Wales c. 1975
nla.cat-vn4227577

80–81
William Yang (b. 1943)
Brett Whiteley 1975
reproduction
My Generation series
nla.obj-326457609

82
Stuart Devlin (1931–2018)
Design for the Order of Australia Award c. 1975
Courtesy the Office of the Official Secretary to the Governor-General

83
Department of Social Security
Medibank and You
Canberra: Australian Government Publishing Services, 1975
nla.cat-vn68648

84
G. Forster
Visit the fabulous Hook Island underwater coral observatory on Australia's Great Barrier Reef
Australia: Ansett Airlines, c. 1960s
nla.obj-133647519

85
Gurindji campaign c. 1975
Papers of Frank Hardy 1931–1988
nla.cat-vn2060293

86
Mervyn Bishop (b. 1945)
Prime Minister Gough Whitlam pours soil into the hand of Gurindji Traditional Landowner Vincent Lingiari at Daguragu [Wattie Creek], Northern Territory 1975
reproduction
Mervyn Bishop collection of photographs, 1963–89
Courtesy Mervyn Bishop and Josef Lebovic Gallery, Sydney
Copyright Commonwealth of Australia, National Indigenous Australians Agency
nla.obj-153513023

87
'Real land rights or political gimmick?: The Northern Territory land rights bill'
c. 1975
Papers of Frank Hardy 1931–1988
nla.cat-vn2060293

89
Robert McFarlane (1942–2023)
Newspaper vendor holding a copy of the Daily Mirror with the headline 'Kerr sacks Gough!', Martin Place, Sydney 1975
reproduction
Robert McFarlane collection of photographs
nla.obj-152388014

90 (top)
Unknown photographer
The Governor-General's official secretary reads the proclamation dissolving parliament on the steps of Parliament House, Canberra 1975
Courtesy the Australian Information Service
nla.obj-147272593

90 (bottom)
Unknown photographer
Malcolm Fraser at Parliament House, Canberra 1975
nla.cat-vn2204202

91
Rick Amor (b. 1948)
Nov 11: Rally Treasury Gardens 1976
Courtesy the artist and Niagara Galleries, Melbourne
nla.cat-vn6938151

Published by National Library of Australia Publishing
Canberra ACT 2600

ISBN: 9781922507914

The National Library of Australia acknowledges First Australians as the Traditional Owners and Custodians of this land and pays respect to Elders—past and present—and through them to all Aboriginal and Torres Strait Islander peoples.

First Nations Peoples are advised this book contains depictions and names of deceased people, and content that may be considered culturally sensitive.

Publisher: Lauren Smith
Authors: Dr Guy Hansen, Peter Appleton, Dr Grace Blakeley-Carroll, Shelly McGuire, Allister Mills, Dr Karen Schamberger, Nicole Schwirtlich
Managing editor: Amelia Hartney
Editorial assistance: Madeleine Warburton
Editor: Dr Robert Nichols
Designer: Amy Cullen (internals), Virginia Buckingham (cover)
Printed in Australia by CanPrint on FSC®-certified paper

Find out more about NLA Publishing at library.gov.au/discover/nla-publishing
A catalogue record for this book is available from the National Library of Australia.